How to Use This Book

Look for these special features in this book:

SIDEBARS, **CHARTS**, **GRAPHS**, and original **MAPS** expand your understanding of what's being discussed—and also make useful sources for classroom reports.

FAQs answer common **F**requently **A**sked **Q**uestions about people, places, and things.

WOW FACTORS offer "Who knew?" facts to keep you thinking.

TRAVEL GUIDE gives you tips on exploring the state—either in person or right from your chair!

PROJECT ROOM provides fun ideas for school assignments and incredible research projects. Plus, there's a guide to primary sources—what they are and how to cite them.

Please note: All statistics are as up-to-date as possible at the time of publication. Population data is taken from the 2010 census.

Consultants: Lesley-Ann L. Dupigny Giroux, Associate Professor and Vermont State Climatologist, University of Vermont; William Loren Katz; Paul M. Searls, Professor of History, University of Vermont

Book production by The Design Lab

Library of Congress Cataloging-in-Publication Data
Heinrichs, Ann.
  Vermont / by Ann Heinrichs. — Revised edition.
    pages cm. — (America the beautiful, third series)
  Includes bibliographical references and index.
  Audience: Ages 9–12.
  ISBN 978-0-531-28296-0 (library binding : alk. paper)
  1. Vermont—Juvenile literature. I. Title.
  F49.3.H45 2014
  974.3—dc23   2013046228

1 2 3 4 5 6 7 8 9 10 R 24 23 22 21 20 19 18 17 16 15

Revised Edition

AMERICA ★ THE ★ BEAUTIFUL

Vermont

BY ANN HEINRICHS

Third Series, Revised Edition

Children's Press®
An Imprint of Scholastic Inc.
New York ★ Toronto ★ London ★ Auckland ★ Sydney
Mexico City ★ New Delhi ★ Hong Kong
Danbury, Connecticut

CONTENTS

1 LAND

From the sparkling ripples on Lake Champlain to the craggy peaks of the Green Mountains to the rolling pastures of the Connecticut River valley, Vermont is a place of great natural beauty. **8**

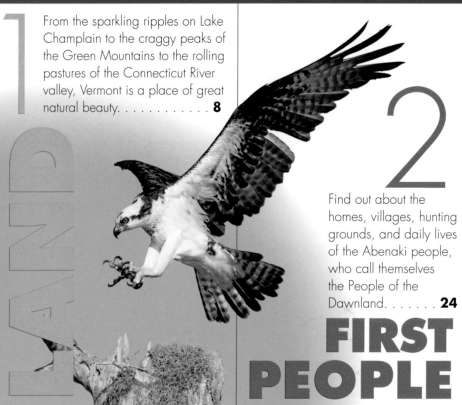

2 FIRST PEOPLE

Find out about the homes, villages, hunting grounds, and daily lives of the Abenaki people, who call themselves the People of the Dawnland. **24**

3 EXPLORATION AND SETTLEMENT

The French and British fight over Vermont. Then Vermonters wage their own battle to become an independent republic. . . . **32**

6 PEOPLE

Learn about the small-town character of Vermont, and see how the state's diverse residents weave their many traditions into Vermont life. **68**

7 GOVERNMENT

Get to the heart of Vermont's state government. At town meetings across rural Vermont, citizens have their say in government. . . . **84**

8 ECONOMY

Maple syrup, computer chips, cheese, granite, and ski resorts all play a part in keeping Vermont's economy humming. **96**

GROWTH AND CHANGE 4

Vermont becomes the 14th U.S. state. Tough Vermonters live by farming, logging, mining, and milling. The state's growing industries attract waves of immigrants. . . . **44**

MORE MODERN TIMES

5

The early 20th century brings upheaval, while in the 21st century, Vermonters face the challenge of balancing economic development and environmental protection. **58**

9 TRAVEL GUIDE

Explore the snowy mountains, nature trails, historic sites, and picturesque villages of the Green Mountain State. **104**

PROJECT ROOM

★

PROJECTS. 116

TIMELINE 122

GLOSSARY 125

FAST FACTS 126

BIOGRAPHICAL DICTIONARY . . 133

RESOURCES 138

★

INDEX 139

AUTHOR'S TIPS AND
SOURCE NOTES 143

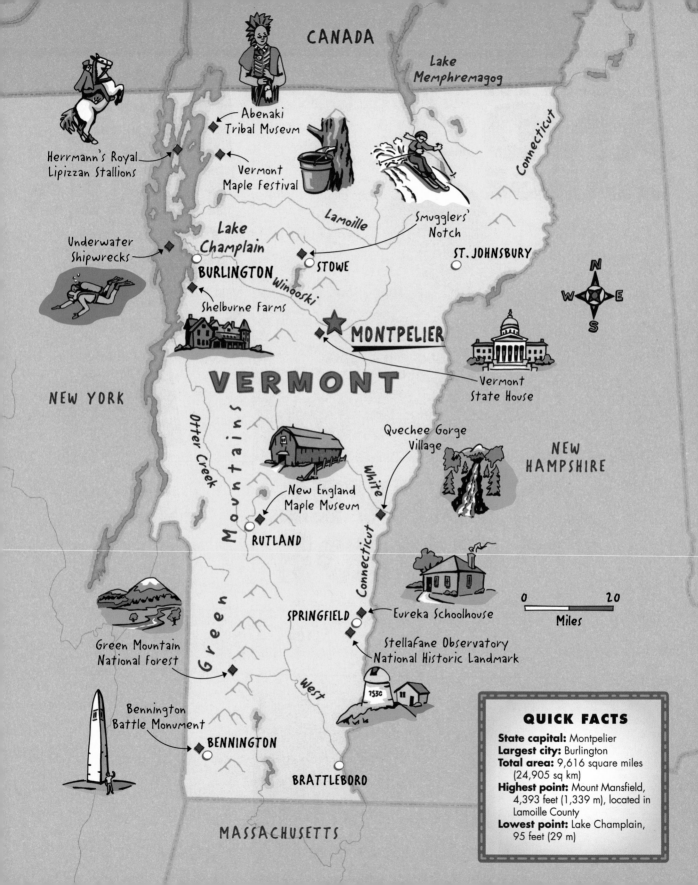

CANADA

Lake
Memphremagog

Herrmann's Royal
Lipizzan Stallions

Abenaki
Tribal Museum

Vermont
Maple Festival

Lamoille

Smugglers'
Notch

ST. JOHNSBURY

Connecticut

Lake
Champlain

Underwater
Shipwrecks

BURLINGTON

STOWE

Winooski

N
W   E
S

MONTPELIER

Shelburne Farms

Vermont
State House

NEW YORK

VERMONT

Otter Creek

Green Mountains

New England
Maple Museum

Quechee Gorge
Village

White

NEW
HAMPSHIRE

Connecticut

RUTLAND

0   20
Miles

Green Mountain
National Forest

SPRINGFIELD

Eureka Schoolhouse

Stellafane Observatory
National Historic Landmark

West

Bennington
Battle Monument

BENNINGTON

BRATTLEBORO

QUICK FACTS

State capital: Montpelier
Largest city: Burlington
Total area: 9,616 square miles
(24,905 sq km)
Highest point: Mount Mansfield,
4,393 feet (1,339 m), located in
Lamoille County
Lowest point: Lake Champlain,
95 feet (29 m)

MASSACHUSETTS

Welcome to Vermont!

HOW DID VERMONT GET ITS NAME?

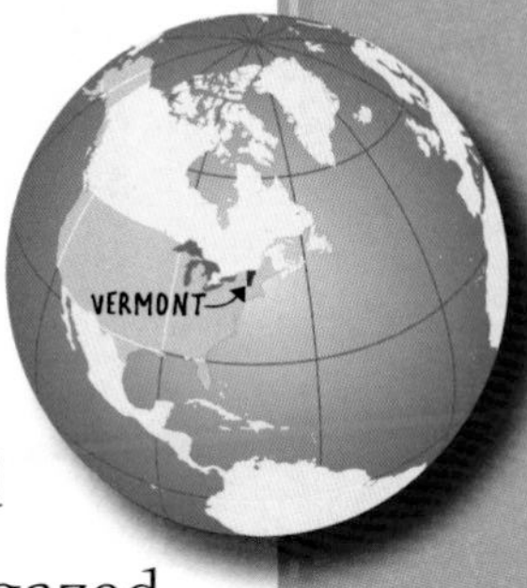

The story of Vermont's name begins in 1609. Frenchman Samuel de Champlain ventured out from Canada, just north of today's Vermont. He followed waterways into a lake that would be named after him—Lake Champlain. As he gazed around this land, he saw forested peaks in the distance. It was these mountains that eventually earned Vermont its name, as the words *verts monts* are French for "green mountains."

VERMONT

ATLANTIC
OCEAN

8

READ ABOUT

Building Mountains . . . 12

Land Regions 12

Vermont Weather 18

Plant Life 20

Animal Life . . . 21

Protecting the Environment . . . 22

Moss Glen Falls in the Green Mountains

CHAPTER ONE

LAND

★

VERMONT IS ONE OF THE SMALLEST STATES IN THE COUNTRY. It covers only 9,616 square miles (24,905 square kilometers). The state's highest point is Mount Mansfield, rising 4,393 feet (1,339 meters) in the Green Mountains. If you stand atop this peak, you can see Vermont's lowest point in the distance. That's Lake Champlain, at 95 feet (29 m) above sea level. Though Vermont is small, within its borders you'll find thick forests, scenic mountains, sandy lakeshores, and fertile river valleys.

The Windsor–Cornish Covered Bridge crosses the Connecticut River at the Vermont–New Hampshire border.

WHERE IS VERMONT?

Vermont is located in the northeast corner of the United States. It's one of the six New England states. (The others are Maine, New Hampshire, Massachusetts, Rhode Island, and Connecticut.) Vermont is the only New England state that does not border the Atlantic Ocean.

New Hampshire lies east of Vermont, with the Connecticut River separating the two. To the south is Massachusetts. New York State is west of Vermont, with Lake Champlain forming much of their border. If you travel north of Vermont, you will enter another country. Canada's province of Quebec lies across Vermont's northern border.

Vermont Topography

Use the color-coded elevation chart to see on the map Vermont's high points (dark red to orange) and low points (green). Elevation is measured as the distance above or below sea level.

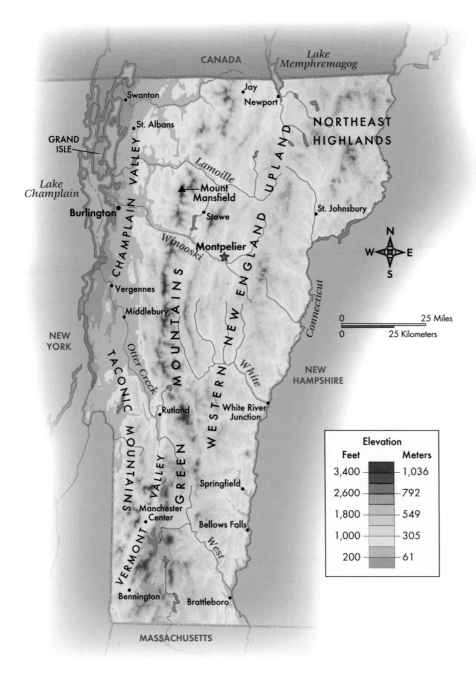

CANADA

Lake Memphremagog

Swanton

Jay
Newport

St. Albans

NORTHEAST HIGHLANDS

GRAND ISLE

CHAMPLAIN VALLEY

Lamoille

UPLAND

Lake Champlain

Mount Mansfield

Stowe

St. Johnsbury

Burlington

Winooski

Montpelier

NEW ENGLAND

N
W   E
S

Vergennes

Middlebury

Connecticut

MOUNTAINS

0   25 Miles
0   25 Kilometers

NEW YORK

Otter Creek

WESTERN

White

NEW HAMPSHIRE

TACONIC MOUNTAINS

Rutland

GREEN

White River Junction

Elevation		
Feet		Meters
3,400		1,036
2,600		792
1,800		549
1,000		305
200		61

Springfield

VERMONT VALLEY

Manchester Center

Bellows Falls

West

Bennington

Brattleboro

MASSACHUSETTS

Vermont Geo-Facts

Along with the state's geographical highlights, this chart ranks Vermont's land, water, and total area compared to all other states.

Total area; rank . . . . 9,616 square miles (24,905 sq km); 45th
Land; rank . . . . .9,217 square miles (23,872 sq km); 43rd
Water; rank . . . . 400 square miles (1,036 sq km); 46th
Inland water; rank . . . . .400 square miles (1,036 sq km); 41st
Geographic center . . . . In Washington County, 3 miles (5 km) east of Roxbury
Latitude . . . . 42°44' N to 45°0'43" N
Longitude . . . . 71°28' W to 73°26' W
Highest point . . . . Mount Mansfield, 4,393 feet (1,339 m), in Lamoille County
Lowest point . . . . Lake Champlain, 95 feet (29 m)
Largest city . . . . Burlington
Longest river . . . . Otter Creek, 100 miles (161 km)

Source: U.S. Census Bureau, 2010 census

Vermont could fit inside Alaska, the largest state, 69 times!

BUILDING MOUNTAINS

Earth's surface is broken up into several gigantic pieces called tectonic plates. These giant landmasses are always shifting. Some pull away from each other, while others collide. In what is now Vermont, two of these giant plates pulled apart about 500 million years ago. Seawater filled the gap, creating a shallow ocean.

As the two plates moved back toward each other, one began to slip beneath the other and thrust up a chain of islands, which included most of today's New England. Further collisions about 425 million years ago formed the Taconic Mountains. By about 390 million years ago, the two giant plates had drifted back together, closing up the ocean and forming the Green Mountains.

These are just a few of the many geological events that helped shape Vermont's rugged landscape. Changes in the climate also played a part. A series of ice ages began about 2 million years ago, and glaciers, or massive rivers of ice, covered the land. As the last of the glaciers began to melt about 20,000 years ago, their waters began spreading to the Champlain Valley, where Lake Champlain is today.

LAND REGIONS

Geographers divide Vermont into six land regions. They are the Northeast Highlands, the Green Mountains, the

A marina on Lake Memphremagog

Western New England Upland, the Taconic Mountains, the Vermont Valley, and the Champlain Valley.

The Northeast Highlands

The Northeast Highlands region is in far northeastern Vermont, reaching eastward into New Hampshire and Maine. This rough, wild region of high, granite mountains and swift-running streams is sparsely populated. Vermont's second-largest lake, Lake Memphremagog, reaches from this region across the border into Canada.

The Green Mountains

The densely forested Green Mountains run like a backbone down the center of the state. They are part of the Appalachian Mountain range, which reaches from Maine

The summit of Mount Mansfield, Vermont's highest point

SEE IT HERE!

GREEN MOUNTAIN NATIONAL FOREST

Green Mountain National Forest was established in 1932 after uncontrolled logging had destroyed much of the state's forestland. Today, the forest stretches across about two-thirds of Vermont and covers more than 350,000 acres (142,000 hectares). Its diverse landscapes range from the rugged peaks of the Green Mountains to ponds, brooks, and wilderness meadows. Its thickets of maple, birch, and pine trees provide cover for moose, deer, and bears.

to Alabama. The Green Mountains stretch through Vermont for about 250 miles (402 km), reaching all the way from the Massachusetts border in the south to Canada in the north. Mount Mansfield, Vermont's highest point, is one of the many craggy peaks in these mountains. Others are Killington Peak, Mount Ellen, Camel's Hump, and Mount Wilson. In the north, the Missisquoi, Winooski, and Lamoille rivers cut deep valleys through the mountains as they flow westward toward Lake Champlain.

The Green Mountains (or *Verts Monts* in French) gave Vermont its nickname, the Green Mountain State. They once formed a barrier to travel between eastern and western Vermont. Today, the Green Mountains are a popular destination for snow skiers. Hikers make their way along the mountains, too, taking a wilderness trail called the Long Trail.

Vermont National Park Areas

This map shows some of Vermont's national parks, trails, sites, and other areas protected by the National Park Service.

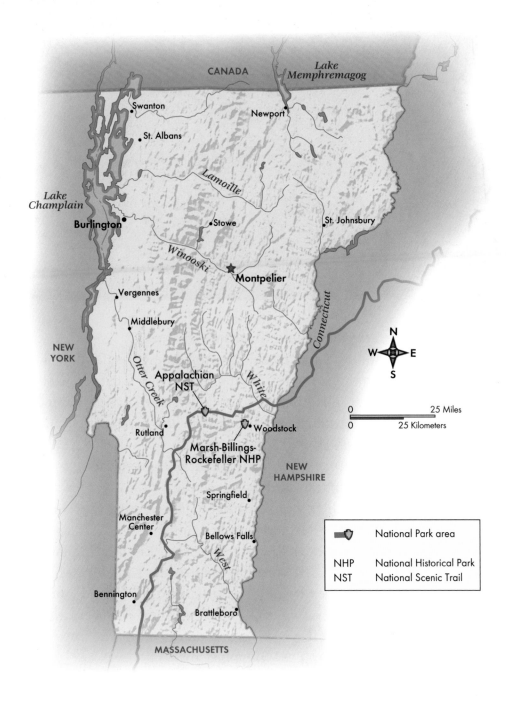

CANADA

Lake Memphremagog

Swanton

Newport

St. Albans

Lamoille

Lake Champlain

Stowe

St. Johnsbury

Burlington

Winooski

★ **Montpelier**

Vergennes

Middlebury

Connecticut

NEW YORK

Appalachian NST

Otter Creek

White

N

W E

S

Rutland

Woodstock

Marsh-Billings-Rockefeller NHP

NEW HAMPSHIRE

0   25 Miles

0   25 Kilometers

Springfield

Manchester Center

Bellows Falls

West

		National Park area
NHP		National Historical Park
NST		National Scenic Trail

Bennington

Brattleboro

MASSACHUSETTS

Picking apples in a Vermont orchard

The Western New England Upland

The rolling land of the Western New England Upland is Vermont's largest region, covering most of eastern Vermont. The upland gradually slopes down from the Green Mountains in the west to the Connecticut River in the east. This region is sometimes called the Vermont Piedmont (*piedmont* means "foot of the mountains").

The hills around Barre contain granite. This area's granite industry has thrived for centuries. Nearby, Montpelier is Vermont's state capital.

The northern part of the New England Upland is sometimes called Vermont's Northeast Kingdom because of the stark beauty of its mountains, forests, and streams. Farther south is a rich farming area. Farmers in the Connecticut River valley raise dairy cattle and crops such as tomatoes, apples, and tobacco.

The Taconic Mountains

The Taconic Mountains region lies in southwest Vermont. It extends into Vermont from New York State. Mount Equinox, near Manchester, is the highest peak in the Taconics. This region contains large deposits of marble and slate, and Rutland has long been a center of the marble industry.

The Vermont Valley

The Vermont Valley is a narrow strip of land in southern Vermont near the western border. It lies between the Taconic Mountains to the west and the Green Mountains to the east. Waterways such as Otter Creek, Batten Kill, and the Walloomsac River rush through the valley. Here, as in the Taconics, marble **quarrying** is an important industry. Sometimes called the Valley of Vermont, this strip was an entry point for many early European settlers. They traveled northward into the valley from Massachusetts and other New England states.

The Champlain Valley

The Champlain Valley, which is sometimes called the Vermont Lowland, is a rolling lowland that lies between the Green and Taconic mountains to the east and Lake Champlain to the west. Fertile soils here make it a rich farming region. Farmers in the valley raise dairy cattle, fruit trees, and field crops. The area around Burlington, Vermont's largest city, is highly developed with businesses and homes.

Burlington sits on the shore of Lake Champlain, the state's largest lake. It is sometimes called America's Sixth Great Lake. Although Vermont has no ocean coastline, Lake Champlain's shore is often called New England's West Coast. Vermont shares Lake Champlain with New York

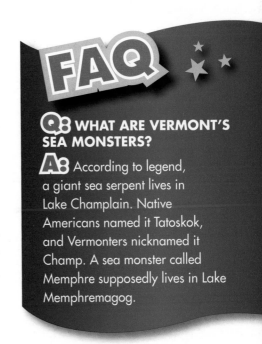

FAQ

Q8 WHAT ARE VERMONT'S SEA MONSTERS?

A8 According to legend, a giant sea serpent lives in Lake Champlain. Native Americans named it Tatoskok, and Vermonters nicknamed it Champ. A sea monster called Memphre supposedly lives in Lake Memphremagog.

WORD TO KNOW

quarrying *extracting stone or minerals from an open-pit mine*

MINI-BIO

GEORGE PERKINS MARSH: EARLY ENVIRONMENTALIST

As a child in Woodstock, George Perkins Marsh (1801–1882) often rode with his father through the woods. His father taught him the name of each tree species, and George never forgot them. In his 1864 book *Man and Nature*, Marsh warned about the devastating effects of humans on the environment. This helped lead to the modern conservation movement as well as the creation of the U.S. National Forest system. He is considered one of America's first environmentalists.

? **Want to know more?** Visit www.factsfornow .scholastic.com and enter the keyword **Vermont**.

Weather Report

This chart shows record temperatures (high and low) for the state, as well as average temperatures (July and January) and average annual precipitation.

Record high temperature . . . . 107°F (42°C) at Vernon on July 7, 1912
Record low temperature . . . . –50°F (–46°C) at Bloomfield on December 30, 1933
Average July temperature, Burlington . . . . 71°F (22°C)
Average January temperature, Burlington . . . . 19°F (–7°C)
Average yearly precipitation, Burlington . . 37 inches (94 cm)

Source: National Climatic Data Center, NESDIS, NOAA, U.S. Department of Commerce

and Quebec. Dozens of islands are scattered in the lake. The largest is South Hero Island, which is home to about 2,000 people.

VERMONT WEATHER

Vermonters like to say that they have different seasons from the rest of the country. Instead of the normal four seasons, they have usual winter, winter, still winter, and mud season. And, really, there are two mud seasons. One is in the spring, from April through May, when the winter snows are melting, making the ground mushy with mud. The other is in late October, when light, early snow melts, creating more mud. Many hiking trails close during the mud seasons because they're too slippery to be safe.

Vermont's winters are long and cold, with the northeast corner (known as the Northeast Kingdom) having the most frigid temperatures. Bloomfield recorded the state's lowest-ever temperature on December 30, 1933, plunging to –50 degrees Fahrenheit (–46 degrees Celsius). The Green Mountains get the most snow, averaging more than 80 inches (203 centimeters).

A snow-covered farm in Woodstock

Winter is when people head to the mountains for skiing and other snow-related sports.

Summers in Vermont are short and warm, though temperatures rarely get too hot. The Champlain Valley experiences the warmest summer temperatures. In the mountains, summer nights can be quite cool. In a rare heat wave, the town of Vernon reached a record high of 107°F (42°C) on July 7, 1912. Fall brings the changing leaves, and people explore the countryside to enjoy the brilliant colors.

THE YEAR WITHOUT A SUMMER

The year 1816 is legendary in Vermont's history. Cold fronts swept across the state throughout the summer and fall, bringing icy blasts and heavy snows. Crops withered and trees lost their leaves. Again and again, farmers replanted their crops, but each time, the killing frost laid waste to their fields. As a result, many Vermonters migrated west during what was called the Year Without a Summer.

What caused the frigid weather? Scientists believe it was a volcano. In April 1815, the Mount Tambora volcano in what is now Indonesia erupted for six straight days. It blasted an estimated 36 cubic miles (150 cubic km) of dust and ash into the atmosphere—more than any other volcano in recorded history. The debris encircled the earth, blocking the sun's rays and causing low temperatures, crop failures, and famine worldwide.

PLANT LIFE

More than three-fourths of Vermont is covered with forests. Conifers, or cone-bearing trees, grow in the mountains. They include pine, spruce, cedar, fir, and hemlock trees. Other common trees are ash, basswood, beech, birch, elm, hickory, maple, oak, and poplar. They are deciduous trees, meaning they lose their leaves in the winter.

Vermont's official state tree is the sugar maple. People use its sap to make delicious maple syrup. It also makes the most colorful autumn spectacle, exploding with brilliant reds, oranges, and golds. Sugar maple trees produce colorful leaves wherever they grow, but Vermont's particular climate and soil conditions make for even more spectacular colors.

Dozens of types of ferns grow in Vermont. They flourish in shady, moist soil. One is the fiddlehead fern, whose leaves form a curly spiral before they open up. Some people gather fiddleheads and cook them. Wildflowers carpet the meadows and mountainsides in the spring. They include anemones, buttercups, daisies, goldenrods, and violets. Flowering bushes such as lilacs and pussy willows also flourish in Vermont.

Sugar maples in brilliant autumn color

Bobcats make their homes in Vermont forests.

ANIMAL LIFE

White-tailed deer are one of Vermont's most abundant wild animal species. They live almost everywhere in the state. Black bears inhabit the woods, and the moose population is growing. Wild cats such as bobcats live in the forests, too, but they're rarely seen. Smaller animals that make their homes in the forest are foxes, minks, muskrats, raccoons, skunks, rabbits, squirrels, woodchucks, and porcupines.

Rivers, streams, lakes, and ponds abound with salmon and trout. Other common fish are bass, pike, perch, pickerel, and smelt. Robins, redwing blackbirds, sparrows, and blue jays flit through the trees in the spring and summer. In the winter, you'll see chickadees, juncos, and nuthatches. Birds that stay near the ground include wild turkeys, ruffed grouse, ring-necked pheasants, and woodcocks. Lakes, rivers, and ponds are nesting sites for ducks and geese.

Zebra mussels are a big problem in Lake Champlain. These little shellfish are an example of an **invasive species**. Native to central Asia and eastern Europe,

WORD TO KNOW

invasive species *wildlife that is not native to a region and harms native plants or animals*

ENDANGERED SPECIES

Vermont lists a number of species as **endangered** or **threatened**. Many of these species live in or around Lake Champlain. Several types of mussels are endangered because zebra mussels are eating their food or smothering them. Other endangered species include the common tern, a seabird that has declined because of predators, overcrowded nesting sites, and human activity. Conservation efforts have helped it begin to make a comeback. Another bird, the osprey, almost disappeared across the nation because of the use of pesticides, chemicals used to kill insects. The pesticides ended up in fish, the ospreys' main food. After eating the poisoned fish, the ospreys seldom produced healthy eggs. In Vermont today, protection efforts are bringing back these magnificent birds, and the species was removed from the state's threatened and endangered list in 2005.

WORDS TO KNOW

endangered *at risk of becoming extinct*

threatened *likely to become endangered in the foreseeable future*

clear-cutting *a type of logging in which all of the trees in an area are cut down*

erosion *the gradual wearing away of rock or soil by physical breakdown, chemical solution, or water*

Ospreys have benefited from protection efforts. Now they live throughout Vermont.

they were accidentally transported to North America on ships. Zebra mussels live in colonies of up to 65,000 mussels per square foot (700,000 per sq m). They clog the pipes that supply water to homes, factories, and farms. They also attach themselves to boat hulls and motors, and their sharp shells can injure swimmers. Native mussels are declining as zebra mussels eat their food supply. Vermont officials are working on ways to control zebra mussels. The state now requires that they be cleaned off boats that are entering or leaving Lake Champlain.

PROTECTING THE ENVIRONMENT

Vermonters have worked hard to protect their natural resources. In the late 19th century, just 30 percent of Vermont land remained forested. Loggers had stripped much of the land bare using **clear-cutting**. This led to soil **erosion**, because without the tree roots to anchor the soil in place, it simply washed away. And without soil to soak into, water rushed across the land, producing floods.

A devastating flood hit Vermont in 1927, killing 84 people and washing out 1,200 bridges.

To help protect Vermont's remaining forestland, the government created the Green Mountain National Forest in 1932. Vermonters also enacted controls on clear-cutting. In 1970, the state passed a law that put strict limits on developments such as shopping centers, making sure that they don't do much harm to the environment.

Pollution from factories and power plants has been a big concern in Vermont. Harmful chemicals float into the atmosphere and then create **acid rain** when they dissolve in precipitation. The acid rain damages trees, pollutes lakes and rivers, kills fish, and endangers other wildlife. Vermonters have managed to drastically reduce the amount of hazardous chemicals released into their water and air.

Today, many different organizations are working to protect Vermont's environment. Vermont's Department of Environmental Conservation monitors air and water quality. The Department of Fish and Wildlife oversees animals and plants and protects their habitats. The Vermont Natural Resources Council is Vermont's branch of the National Wildlife Federation. Its members work for clean air and water and healthy forests. Vermonters have formed many other citizens' organizations to address environmental concerns. They hope to keep their state clean, natural, and beautiful for generations to come.

MINI-BIO

MEERI ZETTERSTROM: GRANDMA OSPREY

When Meeri Zetterstrom (1921–2010) was growing up in Finland, she saw thousands of ospreys diving into the water to catch fish. Eventually, she moved into a log cabin on the shore of Arrowhead Mountain Lake, near Milton, Vermont. There she saw one osprey, but it soon disappeared. Zetterstrom pressured state and local officials to create a protection zone and nesting sites for ospreys. People began calling her Grandma Osprey. In time, the osprey population around the lake made a comeback.

? **Want to know more?** Visit www.factsfornow.scholastic.com and enter the keyword **Vermont**.

WORD TO KNOW

acid rain *pollution that falls to the earth in the form of precipitation*

READ ABOUT

Archaic and
Woodland
Cultures 26

People of the
Dawnland 26

Abenaki
Villages 28

Daily Life 29

Spirituality and
Society 30

Paleo-Indian hunters prepare the meat and hide from a caribou.

Tool made from a deer antler

c. 14,000 BCE
People enter North America from Asia

c. 9000 BCE
Paleo-Indians begin hunting in today's Vermont

▲ c. 7000 BCE
The Archaic culture develops

CHAPTER TWO

FIRST PEOPLE

★

HUMANS FIRST CROSSED FROM ASIA INTO NORTH AMERICA AT LEAST 16,000 YEARS AGO. Called Paleo-Indians, they moved across the continent pursuing herds of large animals such as caribou, a type of reindeer. Paleo-Indians also gathered plants to eat. Traveling in small bands of 25 to 30 people, they eventually reached the Vermont region about 11,000 years ago.

Abenaki mask

c. 4000 BCE
The climate warms and the population grows

c. 1000 BCE
People begin hunting with bows and arrows and making clay pottery

c. 1600 CE ▲
About 6,000 Abenakis live in Vermont

ARCHAIC AND WOODLAND CULTURES

By about 9,000 years ago, the climate began to warm. Animals and plants much like today's species appeared, and people adapted to their new surroundings. By 8,000 years ago, they were living in larger, more stable communities. They hunted with stone-tipped spears, fished, and gathered wild plants, moving as the seasons and food supplies changed. **Archaeologists** call this the Archaic Period.

By around 4000 BCE, the climate warmed and forests flourished. The population also grew. Around 3,000 years ago, people began settling in more permanent villages. This is the beginning of the Woodland Period. Woodland peoples cleared fields around their villages and cultivated crops. They also fashioned pottery from clay. For hunting, they used bows and arrows.

PEOPLE OF THE DAWNLAND

Eventually, people organized themselves into groups. One group called itself the Alnôbak, meaning "people." This group is now known as Abenakis. Their land, which stretched across what are now northern New England and southern Quebec, was called *Ndakinna*, which means "our land." The Abenaki people eventually joined with other groups. Often called the Wabanaki Confederacy, this **alliance** was formed as a defense against frequent raids by the aggressive Iroquois of today's upper New York State. Other groups that lived in the region included Mohicans and Pennacooks.

Western Abenakis occupied all of present-day Vermont, as well as New Hampshire. They were divided into several groups, each with its own territorial hunting and fishing grounds. Missisquois lived on the eastern shore of Lake Champlain, and Sokokis lived alongside the

WORDS TO KNOW

archaeologists *people who study the remains of past human societies*

alliance *an association among groups that benefits all the members*

Native American Peoples

(Before European Contact)

This map shows the general area of Native American peoples before European settlers arrived.

A Native American canoeing on Lake Champlain

Missisquoi River near the lake and in the Connecticut River Valley. Cowasucks lived along the Connecticut River. About 6,000 Abenakis lived in Vermont in the 1600s.

ABENAKI VILLAGES

Vermont's Abenaki people laid out their villages along riverbanks. Members of an extended family settled together in groups of 50 to 100 people. Near Newbury and Swanton, archaeologists have found villages that housed as many as 500 people.

Abenakis lived in dome-shaped homes called wigwams. They built these dwellings by bending saplings, or young trees, to form a frame, which they covered with bark or woven mats. A central fireplace provided warmth,

Q8 HOW DID ABENAKIS KEEP TRACK OF TIME THROUGHOUT THE YEAR?

A8 Abenakis followed a lunar, or moon-based, calendar. Each month began with the new moon and was named for the events that came with the season. For example, the Planter Moon was in May, the Harvesting Moon was in August, the Leaf Falling Moon was in October, and the Winter Maker Moon was in December.

and smoke escaped through a hole in the roof. One or sometimes two families lived in each wigwam. These sturdy structures would last for years. Abenakis also built longhouses—long versions of wigwams.

Abenakis cleared the land around their villages for farming by cutting and burning the trees. There they grew corn, beans, and squash. After harvesting the crops, they preserved much of the food to eat during the winter. They used river water for cooking, bathing, and watering their fields.

DAILY LIFE

Men used bows and arrows to hunt deer, moose, and other wild animals in the forests. They caught smaller animals with traps. They ate some meat right away and smoked other meat to preserve it. The furry skins became warm cloaks and blankets. Men also made canoes from the strong bark of the birch tree, sealing the seams with pitch, or sticky pine sap. They caught fish in the river using nets, traps, and spears. Fish were split open and arranged on wooden racks to dry. The dried fish were set aside for the winter. Men brought younger boys along on their hunting and fishing expeditions. They taught the children to respect the natural world and the gifts it provided.

Women cared for children, harvested crops, and cooked meals in clay pots. In the surrounding forest, they gathered nuts, berries, and herbs and then hung the wild plants to dry inside the wigwams. Using bark strips and sweetgrass, they wove baskets to hold food and household goods. Women also taught girls to do grown-up tasks.

When winter came, Abenaki groups moved to temporary winter hunting grounds. There they built cone-shaped homes made by covering wooden frames with bark. As winter was coming to an end, Abenakis tapped

SEE IT HERE!

CHIMNEY POINT

The Chimney Point State Historic Site in Addison preserves cultural artifacts of the Abenaki people. Items on display include ceremonial masks, pottery, art, trade goods, weapons, tools, and clothing. Visitors can take an outdoor walking tour and learn how humans first settled in the area more than 9,000 years ago. The museum also offers workshops in Abenaki technology, such as using flint to make weapons and tools. There's even an annual spear-throwing contest in September!

WOW

Abenaki hunters used moose callers to lure moose. They rolled birch bark into a funnel shape and blew into it, making a moose-like call.

Picture Yourself . . .

in an Abenaki Sugar Camp

It's early spring, and snow is still on the ground. The grown-ups have been watching the moon and the weather. They know it's time to go sugaring. You will make maple syrup the way the great hero Gluskabe taught your people long ago.

With your parents and other relatives, you put on your snowshoes and set out from your winter camp. Soon you reach the sugar maple groves, where you set up the sugar camp. Using your sharpened stone knife, you make a V-shaped cut in the maple bark. At the bottom of the cut, you attach a spout made of a hollow reed. On the ground beneath the spout, you place a bark bucket. Soon the sweet, sticky *zogalinebi* (sap) is dripping into the bucket.

On the way back to the camp, you gather wood to set a fire. When it's blazing, you place stones on the fire. Once the stones are hot, you place them in the buckets of maple sap. This boils the water out, leaving the thick, sweet maple syrup you will enjoy all year long.

the sweet sap from maple trees to make maple syrup. When Europeans settled in their territory, the Abenaki people taught this skill to their new neighbors.

SPIRITUALITY AND SOCIETY

The Abenaki people believed in a creator god called Tabaldak. They also honored the spirits of animals, plants, and winds. Thus, animals and plants were to be respected and treated with care. Other spirits of the natural world were Mother Earth, Father Sky, Grandmother Moon, and Grandfather Sun. Abenaki storytellers told tales to instruct children and to reinforce community values. They told many stories about the heroic figure Gluskabe and the foolish raccoon Azban.

The Abenaki people had no central authority. Extended family groups usually governed themselves. The rights to hunting grounds were passed down through the father's side of the family. Each group had a sachem, or spiritual leader. Sometimes, several groups banded together under a powerful sachem to fight wars. But all adults took part in discussing important matters, such as whether to make war or peace.

Parents did not hit their children or yell at them. Instead, they spoke quietly, often telling a traditional tale to make a point about wise behavior.

Abenaki sachems provided spiritual guidance to the Abenaki people.

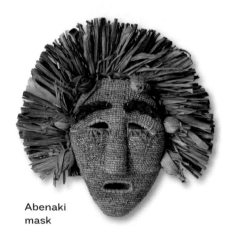

Abenaki mask

READ ABOUT

French and British
Settlements . . . 35

Abenakis and
Settlers 36

The Green
Mountain
Boys 39

An Independent
Republic 40

Surviving in the
Wilderness . . . 41

Samuel de Champlain
and his crew exploring
North America

1609

*French explorer Samuel
de Champlain is the
first European to reach
Vermont*

1666

*The French build Fort
Sainte Anne on Isle
La Motte*

1700s ▲

*European settlers begin
moving to Vermont*

CHAPTER THREE

EXPLORATION AND SETTLEMENT

★

FRENCH PEOPLE WERE THE FIRST EUROPEANS TO REACH PRESENT-DAY VERMONT. The colony of New France lay to the north, where Canada is today. Frenchman Samuel de Champlain had founded Quebec City there. Then he sailed out to acquire more lands. In 1609, he reached what is now called Lake Champlain.

1763

Great Britain gains
control of Vermont
after the French and
Indian War

c. 1770 ►

Ethan Allen organizes
the Green Mountain
Boys to drive New York
settlers out of Vermont

1777

Vermonters declare
Vermont an
independent republic

European Exploration of Vermont

The colored arrows on this map show the route taken by Samuel de Champlain in 1609.

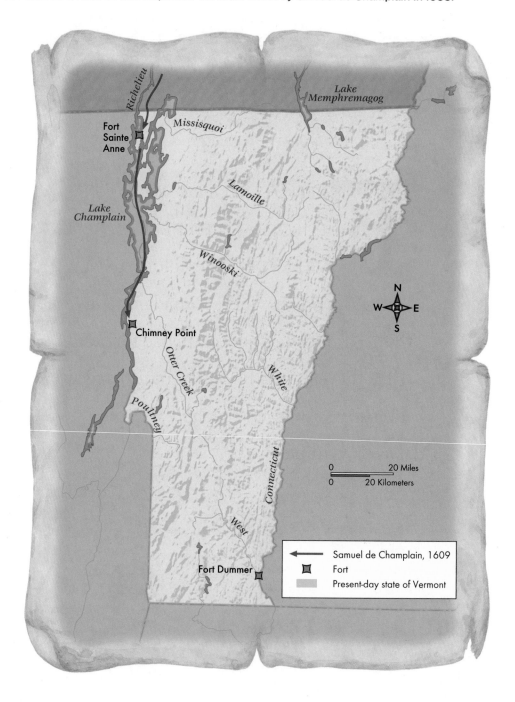

Some of the first visitors to the Vermont region were fur trappers who traded with the Native Americans.

FRENCH AND BRITISH SETTLEMENTS

In 1666, Frenchmen landed on Isle La Motte, an island on Lake Champlain. There they built a settlement called Fort Sainte Anne. It did not last, but Champlain had spread the word about the beautiful forests around the lake. This eventually attracted more Frenchmen, who built homes on the shores of Lake Champlain.

Most of the early French people in Vermont were fur traders and **missionaries**. Roman Catholic priests of the Jesuit order came to teach their religion to Abenakis. They visited Abenaki villages in the Champlain Valley as early as 1615.

Meanwhile, the British were settling in colonies along the Atlantic coast. In 1690, British soldiers established a small fort at Chimney Point, on Lake Champlain near

WORD TO KNOW

missionaries *people who are sent to foreign lands to try to convert others to a religion*

Early settlers in Vermont, traveling along the Connecticut River

today's Addison. Soon settlers from the Massachusetts and Connecticut colonies began moving into Vermont. Some settled along the Connecticut River in the east. Here, in 1724, British soldiers set up Fort Dummer near today's Brattleboro. This would be Vermont's first permanent European settlement. Other settlers entered through the Valley of Vermont, a narrow pass in southwestern Vermont between the Taconic Mountains and the Green Mountains.

ABENAKIS AND SETTLERS

European explorers, traders, trappers, and farmers were moving into Vermont. The Abenaki people helped their new neighbors survive. Some traded beaver furs with the newcomers in exchange for pots and pans, cloth, beads, axes, and other metal tools. Abenakis taught settlers how to tap maple trees.

As more British settlers arrived, the French fought to protect their claims to the region. Rivalry between the two powers eventually led to the French and Indian War (1754–1763). The Abenaki people were caught in the middle of this conflict. Their homeland became a war zone. Some Abenakis sided with the British, but most joined the French. The French generally treated the Abenaki people more fairly than the

Native Americans taught European settlers how to make maple syrup.

HE WHO FOOLS THE OTHERS

Grey Lock (c. 1670–1750) was a Western Abenaki leader. For a time, he lived at Missisquoi Bay, just north of the Vermont border. Grey Lock resented British settlements on Abenaki land. In Dummer's War of the 1720s, he led raids on British settlers in Massachusetts and Vermont. No one could capture him. People called him Wawanolet, meaning "he who fools the others, or puts someone off the track." Other Abenaki leaders made peace with the British, but Grey Lock never did.

Soldiers making their way through forests during the French and Indian War

British did. Besides, the British allied themselves with the Iroquois Nation, long the enemies of the Abenakis.

As British settlers moved in from the south, they pushed hundreds of Abenakis out of their villages. Many villagers fled to Saint Francis, a French mission in Quebec, Canada. Some fled west into New York, while others hid in the wilderness. In the end, Great Britain won the war. Vermont and other French holdings in the region then fell under British control. Abenaki land claims were completely ignored.

THE GREEN MOUNTAIN BOYS

At the end of the war, more white settlers came to Vermont. People from both New York and New Hampshire colonies claimed land there. Between 1749 and 1763, New Hampshire's governor had granted Vermont land to 135 settlers. They called this area the New Hampshire Grants. Not to be outdone, New York's governor had granted the same land to New Yorkers.

Great Britain finally stepped in and declared that New York controlled the disputed area. New York officials then declared that the New Hampshire Grants were not valid. If New Hampshire settlers wanted to stay, they would have to buy New York titles to their land. Naturally, the New Hampshirites weren't eager to leave. That's when Ethan Allen sprang into action. His family had lived in Bennington for years. Around 1770, Allen and others formed an armed military force called the Green Mountain Boys. They harassed New York officials and pressured many New Yorkers into leaving Vermont. For years, the Green Mountain Boys practically ruled Vermont.

Vermonters were still sorting out their land problems when the Revolutionary War began in April 1775. Colonists were fighting this war to win their independence from Great Britain. Just one month later, Ethan Allen mustered his Green Mountain Boys into action again. The British controlled Fort Ticonderoga, across Lake Champlain in New York. On May 10, 1775, the

MINI-BIO

ETHAN ALLEN: FREEDOM FIGHTER

Red-headed and loud-mouthed, Ethan Allen (1738–1789) was a fierce freedom fighter. To many, he was a troublemaker. With his brother Ira and his cousins Seth Warner and Remember Baker, he founded the Green Mountain Boys. Allen and the Green Mountain Boys took Fort Ticonderoga in the Revolutionary War. But the British soon captured Allen during his failed attempt to conquer Montreal, Canada. They held him prisoner until 1778. While he was in jail, Vermont declared itself an independent republic.

? Want to know more? Visit www.factsfornow.scholastic.com and enter the keyword **Vermont**.

WORD TO KNOW

republic *a nation in which the supreme power rests with citizens who can vote*

Ethan Allen and the Green Mountain Boys capturing Fort Ticonderoga in 1775

SEE IT HERE!

OLD CONSTITUTION HOUSE

The Old **Constitution** House in Windsor is known as the birthplace of Vermont. The building used to be Windsor Tavern. Here, on July 8, 1777, Vermonters met and drew up their first constitution. While the delegates were meeting, news came that British troops were on the march nearby. Delegates began to panic and wanted to leave the meeting, but a violent thunderstorm broke out, trapping everyone inside. They were forced to keep working on the constitution until it was finished.

Green Mountain Boys took the fort. The colonists managed to hold the fort until 1777, when the British took it back. Colonial troops retreated, with the British hot on their heels. The two sides clashed at Hubbardton, but the colonists lost.

AN INDEPENDENT REPUBLIC

In 1776, the American colonists had issued their Declaration of Independence. They declared that the colonies were now the United States of America. Settlers in Vermont decided they wanted to be independent, too. They wanted independence not only from Britain, but also from New York and New Hampshire. In January 1777, Vermonters declared Vermont an independent republic, calling it the Republic of New Connecticut. It was sometimes called the Vermont Republic.

Later that year, in July, representatives met at a tavern in Windsor. They changed their republic's name to Vermont. They also drew up a constitution. Among other things, it declared slavery to be against the law. This was the first time slavery was outlawed in the United States. At this time, **plantation** owners in southern states used enslaved Africans as laborers. Some of these enslaved people managed to escape to the north. As an antislavery republic, Vermont allowed these men and women to live there safely.

Meanwhile, the fighting in the Revolutionary War continued. Though Bennington is in Vermont, the Battle of Bennington of August 1777 was actually fought in New York. This time, the British lost. They eventually surrendered at Saratoga, New York, ending the war's land battles in the northern colonies. In 1783, the Revolutionary War formally came to an end. The 13 British colonies became the first 13 states. Vermont was not one of them, though. It was still an independent republic.

SURVIVING IN THE WILDERNESS

Independence was a way of life for Vermonters. They had settled in a remote frontier, far from big-city conveniences. Most had purchased their land without seeing it. Land developers had gone into Massachusetts and other colonies advertising fantastic farming opportunities in Vermont. Often they offered to sell land in plots of 50 to 100 acres (20 to 40 ha). Much of New England was getting

WORDS TO KNOW

constitution *a written document that contains all the governing principles of a state or country*

plantation *a large farm, usually raising one main crop*

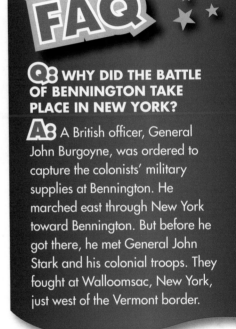

Q8 WHY DID THE BATTLE OF BENNINGTON TAKE PLACE IN NEW YORK?

A8 A British officer, General John Burgoyne, was ordered to capture the colonists' military supplies at Bennington. He marched east through New York toward Bennington. But before he got there, he met General John Stark and his colonial troops. They fought at Walloomsac, New York, just west of the Vermont border.

The Vermont Constitution of 1777 was the first to grant all men the right to vote, regardless of whether they owned property.

Settlers cleared land by using ox and horse teams to plow and pull out tree stumps.

crowded by this time, so Vermont appealed to people who wanted an independent life.

In some cases, the land developers had lied. Far from being fertile, a settler's land might turn out to be rocky or hilly and the soil poor. Moses Warner, one of the first settlers in Andover, arrived from Connecticut in 1776. He bought land that was supposedly great for farming. "He soon found that there were plenty [of stones] underneath the leaves," one of his neighbors wrote, "and the farm is today the most stony one in town."

Life in Vermont was not easy. Most people lived far from their neighbors. They missed the sense of community they had enjoyed before. On their own, families chopped down acres of trees to clear farm-land and build homes. In order to survive, people spent much of their time hunting, fishing, and farming.

Bears and other wild animals posed an ever-present danger. When the winter snows came, settlers worked hard to harvest firewood to cook food and keep warm.

Fewer women than men settled in the rugged wilds of Vermont. Women in Vermont struggled to keep their families fed and clothed. It's no wonder that, in time, Vermonters came to be known for their tough, independent character.

Picture Yourself . . .

in the Vermont Wilderness

Snow blankets the landscape, and chill winds whistle around the log cabin. Stew is boiling in a big, iron kettle over the fireplace. As you glance around the cabin, almost everything you see reminds you of your work in the spring and summer.

You made your dress and your brother Ethan's shirt yourself. You used the flax that grows outside the kitchen door, spinning and weaving it into linen cloth. You made your warm stockings and Ethan's trousers, too. Using your spinning wheel, you spun wool from your family's sheep to make yarn. Then you wove it into woolen cloth on the loom. You churned milk from the cows to make tonight's butter and cheese. You salted the hog's meat to make the bacon and ham.

After supper, you sink into your plump, fluffy feather bed, stuffed with goose feathers. Then you pull the woolen blanket over your head and settle in for warm, cozy sleep.

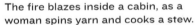

The fire blazes inside a cabin, as a woman spins yarn and cooks a stew.

44

READ ABOUT

Farming and Logging 47

The Birth of New Industries 48

Taking a Stand Against Slavery 51

Industry and Immigration . . 54

Into the 20th Century 56

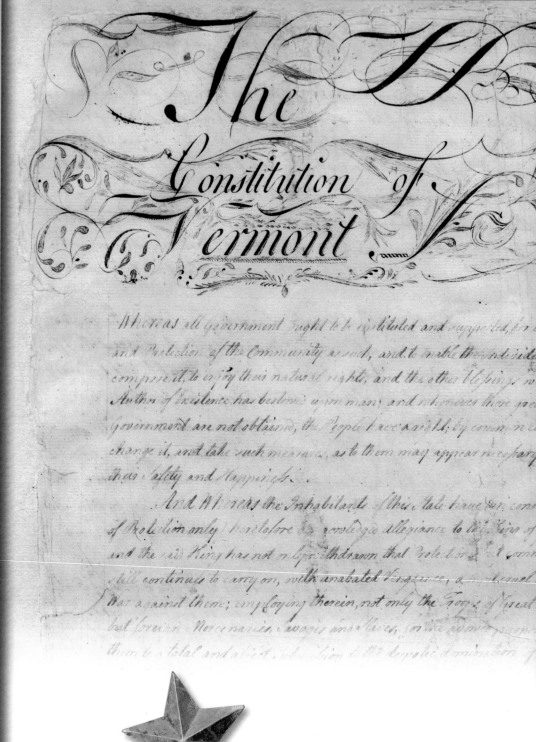

The first page of the original Vermont Constitution

1791 ►
Vermont becomes the 14th U.S. state

c. 1814
Barre's first granite quarry opens

1820
Vermont's legislature passes a resolution against slavery

CHAPTER FOUR

GROWTH AND CHANGE

★

FOR 14 YEARS, VERMONT REMAINED AN INDEPENDENT REPUBLIC. All this time, Vermont and New York continued to quarrel over land rights. Finally, in 1790, Vermont agreed to pay $30,000 to New York to give up its claims. That cleared the way for statehood at last. On March 4, 1791, Vermont became the 14th U.S. state.

1823
The Champlain Canal opens, connecting Lake Champlain with New York's Hudson River

1864
Confederate troops stage the Saint Albans Raid during the Civil War

1918 ▸
Vermont women vote in town elections for the first time

Vermont: From Territory to Statehood
(1777–1791)

This map shows the original Vermont republic and the area (outlined in green) that became the state of Vermont in 1791.

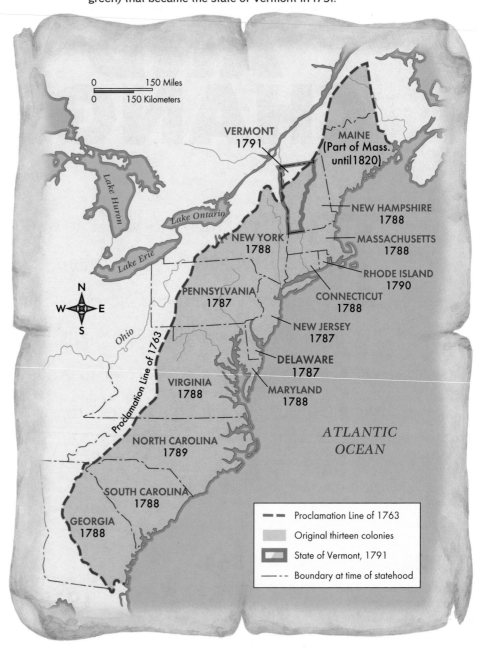

VERMONT
1791

MAINE
(Part of Mass.
until 1820)

NEW HAMPSHIRE
1788

NEW YORK
1788

MASSACHUSETTS
1788

RHODE ISLAND
1790

PENNSYLVANIA
1787

CONNECTICUT
1788

NEW JERSEY
1787

DELAWARE
1787

VIRGINIA
1788

MARYLAND
1788

ATLANTIC
OCEAN

NORTH CAROLINA
1789

SOUTH CAROLINA
1788

GEORGIA
1788

Lake Huron

Lake Ontario

Lake Erie

Ohio

Proclamation Line of 1763

0   150 Miles
0   150 Kilometers

N
W   E
S

- - - Proclamation Line of 1763
      Original thirteen colonies
      State of Vermont, 1791
- - - Boundary at time of statehood

Sheep near a cottage in West Rutland

FARMING AND LOGGING

By the time Vermont became a state, about 85,000 people lived there. Most worked as farmers. They braved long, harsh winters living off their rocky, hilly farms. Many farmers raised beef cattle. Some raised dairy cattle and hogs as well. In 1811, merchant William Jarvis shipped thousands of Merino sheep from Spain to his new farm in Weatherford. Merino sheep were known for their luxurious wool. Soon other farmers began raising Merinos, too. By the 1830s, there were more than a million sheep in Vermont.

Lumber was another thriving industry. Loggers cut thousands of acres of trees. After cutting off the branches,

FREEDOM OF THE PRESS

Matthew Lyon (1749–1822), a poor Irish immigrant, founded the town of Fair Haven in 1783. He fought with the Green Mountain Boys during the Revolutionary War and served in the U.S. Congress. Under the Alien and **Sedition** Acts of 1798, he was jailed for four months for insulting President John Adams in his newspaper, the *Fair Haven Gazette*. While in jail, Lyon was reelected to Congress. Lyon's ordeal stands as a symbol of the importance of the freedom of the press.

WORDS TO KNOW

sedition *conduct or language that stirs up feelings against lawful authority*

textile *cloth or fabric that is woven, knitted, or otherwise manufactured*

wood pulp *ground-up chips or strips of wood*

they hauled the trees over the snow on a sled. When they reached a riverbank or lakeshore, they cut the trees into big logs. In the spring, after the ice had melted, they rolled the logs into the water. Then they floated the logs to other states or to Canada. However, the logging destroyed much of Vermont's ancient forestland. Many wild animals lost their habitats. Without the trees and their roots to hold the rich soil in place, much of it washed away.

THE BIRTH OF NEW INDUSTRIES

In Vermont's early settlements, people made most of what they needed at home. As settlements grew closer together, people developed small-scale industries to serve their growing communities. Craftspeople made useful items for their neighbors in their homes, barns, or shops. Some made shoes, hats, or clothing. Blacksmiths made tools and hardware, and coopers made barrels. Woodworkers made boxes and furniture, and tanners turned raw animal hides into soft leather.

Vermonters also built small, water-powered mills by the rivers and streams. Many early settlements grew up around the mill sites. Some of the earliest mills were sawmills for cutting lumber and gristmills for grinding grain. Sheep farming led to a booming **textile** industry. Many textile mills were built to turn the sheep's wool into yarn.

Vermont's first paper mill had opened in Bennington in 1784. The mill was powered by the falls of the Walloomsac River. At that time, people made paper from cloth rags. But Matthew Lyon of Fair Haven was the first American to make paper out of **wood pulp**. He used his wood-pulp paper mill to make paper for the *Fair Haven Gazette*, a newspaper he founded in 1795.

Quarrying was another new industry. Marble quarries opened in Dorset in 1785 and in Middlebury in the early

Dairy farmers deliver milk to a Vermont cheese factory in the 1870s.

1800s. Granite was found near Barre in the 1790s, and a quarry opened there around 1814. Slate was discovered in southwestern Vermont, too. Workers used hand tools to hack the stone out of the ground. Then they loaded it on oxcarts to transport it. People used granite for fence posts, stair steps, fireplace hearths, and tombstones. They used marble for buildings and statues, and slate for roofs and floors. Vermont's stone quarrying industry would grow to become one of the state's leading industries.

A Vermont marble quarry, 1851

The Champlain Canal transformed Vermont's economy. Opened in 1823, it connected the south end of Lake Champlain with New York's Hudson River. Hundreds of canal boats began to operate on the lake. Now Vermonters could ship stone, lumber, and farm products to New York. On the return trip, they carried manufactured goods and raw materials. It would have cost a fortune to transport all these products overland.

TAKING A STAND AGAINST SLAVERY

African Americans had lived in Vermont since the 1600s, some as enslaved laborers. After Vermont outlawed slavery in 1777, freed blacks became farmers, soldiers, teachers, and ministers. African Americans from other states moved to Vermont, too. In 1791, Vermont had 271 black residents. By 1820, the number of African Americans had risen to 903.

In 1817, Vermonters organized the state chapter of the American Colonization Society. The group's goal was to have enslaved persons returned to their homelands in Africa. Many **abolitionists** saw this as morally wrong. Instead, they favored freeing enslaved people and helping them take their place in American society.

Vermont's legislature passed an antislavery resolution in 1820. It stated that: "Slavery is incompatible with the vital principles of all free governments. . . . It paralyzes industry, . . . stifles the love of freedom, and endangers the safety of the nation. It is prohibited by the laws of nature. . . . The right to introduce and establish slavery in a free government does not exist."

The *Journal of the Times,* an abolitionist newspaper, was published in Bennington. From 1828 to 1829, the abolitionist William Lloyd Garrison was its editor and publisher. Garrison's writings helped persuade Vermonters to form the Vermont Anti-Slavery Society in 1834. By 1836, there were antislavery societies in 89 Vermont towns.

THE PRINCES OF GUILFORD

Abijah Prince was an African American who gained his liberty when he fought for the British in its colonial wars against the French. An employer gave him a 100-acre (40 ha) farm in Guilford, Vermont, and he became one of the original founders of Sunderland. He freed and married Lucy Terry, who had been sold into slavery at age five. Lucy wrote a poem about an armed battle her community had with neighboring Indians, and it became the best-known description of the event. Two of Lucy and Abijah Prince's six children fought in the American Revolution.

When Prince's Guilford farm was attacked by an angry neighbor who tore down fences and set fire to haystacks, Lucy crossed the state on horseback to protest to the Governor's Council. They ruled in her favor.

WORD TO KNOW

abolitionists *people who were opposed to slavery and worked to end it*

William Lloyd Garrison was an editor and publisher who promoted the abolition of slavery.

Many of Vermont's African Americans rose to prominent positions. One was Reverend Lemuel Haynes. He was the pastor of a white congregation at Rutland's West Parish. In the early 1800s, he traveled from church to church preaching about the evils of slavery. Alexander Twilight graduated from Middlebury College in 1823, becoming the first African American in the country to earn a college degree. Martin Henry Freeman of Rutland also graduated from Middlebury College. In 1856, he became president of the Allegheny Institute near Pittsburgh, Pennsylvania. (It later became Avery College.) Freeman was the first black college president in the United States.

Vermonters were also active in the Underground Railroad, a secret network of shelters for people fleeing slavery in the South. "Stationmasters" on the Underground Railroad hid runaways in basements, attics, closets, and secret spaces behind walls. Hundreds of people escaping slavery traveled safely through Vermont to Canada or simply settled in Vermont.

One stop on the Underground Railroad was Rodney Marsh's home in Brandon. It had more than 50 closets for hiding people, eight stairways by which people could flee, and a tunnel from the cellar to the outside. Rowland and Rachel Robinson of Ferrisburgh also helped countless people fleeing slavery.

The dispute over slavery's expansion into western territories eventually led to the Civil War (1861–1865). More than 30,000 Vermonters signed up to fight for the Union, or Northern, side against the Confederates, or Southerners. Among them were about 150 African Americans, more than 20 percent of the state's black population. In 1864, the Saint Albans Raid in northern Vermont was the northernmost land action in the Civil War. The war ended with a Union victory the following year.

MINI-BIO

LEMUEL HAYNES: FREEDOM FIGHTER AND MINISTER

Lemuel Haynes (1753–1833), the son of a black father and a white mother, worked as a servant in Massachusetts until age 21. In Vermont, he marched with Ethan Allen and his Green Mountain Boys when they captured Fort Ticonderoga. After the war, Haynes studied to be a minister. He became the first black minister of a white congregation and preached in a Rutland parish for more than 30 years. Haynes vigorously took part in political arguments and worked to end slavery. In 1804, Middlebury College awarded him an honorary degree, the first ever given to an African American.

? **Want to know more?** Visit www.factsfornow .scholastic.com and enter the keyword **Vermont**.

9th Regiment.
ON TO WASHINGTON !
DOWN WITH THE
REBELLION !
GREEN MOUNTAIN BOYS AWAKE !

I am authorized to recruit for the 9th Regiment of Infantry of Vt. Volunteers. A company is wanted in Caledonia County in 10 days.

Term of Enlistment three years, unless sooner discharged. Pay $23.25 per month and rations.

COME TO THE RESCUE OF OUR GLORIOUS REPUBLIC !

Call at my Office in this Village and information will be given and enlistments made.

THOMAS B. HALL, Rrecruiting Officer.

Groton, June 2, 1862.

This poster encouraged Vermonters to fight in the Civil War.

SEE IT HERE!

ROKEBY MUSEUM

The Rokeby Museum in Ferrisburgh was once the home of Rowland and Rachel Robinson. At their home, the Robinsons welcomed people escaping slavery, let them rest, and educated them before they started their new lives. The Robinsons also gave jobs to some fugitive slaves. At this site, you can stroll around the family farm, one of the largest sheep farms in the region. Many of the original farm buildings are open for viewing.

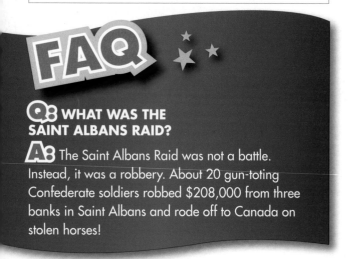

FAQ

Q: WHAT WAS THE SAINT ALBANS RAID?

A: The Saint Albans Raid was not a battle. Instead, it was a robbery. About 20 gun-toting Confederate soldiers robbed $208,000 from three banks in Saint Albans and rode off to Canada on stolen horses!

WORD TO KNOW

machine tools *mechanical devices used to manufacture metal machine parts*

INDUSTRY AND IMMIGRATION

Even though the state remained overwhelmingly rural, some Vermont industries prospered after the war. Lumbering and wood processing kept loggers and sawmill workers busy. The state's dairy cattle made for thriving cheese, butter, and cream industries. In Barre, the granite industry flourished. Workers in Windsor and Springfield manufactured **machine tools**, in Saint Johnsbury they made platform scales, and in Brattleboro they made musical organs. Factories in Bellows Falls made paper. Thousands of immigrants left their homelands to work in Vermont's factories, mills, and quarries.

Immigrants fled their homelands for many reasons. Irish people were starving because disease wiped out crops of potatoes, the basis of their diet, for several years. Jewish people in Russia were being massacred. Other immigrants left because of wars, economic hardship, or rampant diseases.

Some immigrants had special skills they could use in Vermont. Slate mining, for example, was a big industry in Wales, so Welsh miners came to work in Vermont's slate quarries. Italian marble carvers found work in Proctor's marble quarries. Scottish, Italian, Swiss, and Swedish stonecutters came to practice their trade in Barre's granite quarries. African Americans, Canadians, Finns, Poles, Spaniards, and many others made their way to Vermont in the late 1800s.

The E. & T. Fairbanks and Company factory in St. Johnsbury, around 1860

Working conditions were not always good. Railroad workers in Bolton went on **strike** in 1846, and in 1883, miners at the Ely Copper Mines went on strike because they were not being paid their wages. But armed guards came in and ended the strikes. Many workers in the granite quarries got silicosis, a deadly disease caused by inhaling granite particles. Workers organized labor **unions** to force their employers to install dust-removing equipment. By 1900, 90 percent of Barre's granite workers belonged to labor unions.

WORDS TO KNOW

strike *an organized refusal to work, usually as a sign of protest about working conditions*

unions *organizations formed by workers to try to improve working conditions and wages*

MINI-BIO

ANNETTE PARMALEE: SUFFRAGETTE HORNET

Annette Parmalee (1865–1924) got mad when people said that women should not work outside the home. She was so vocal in demanding women's voting rights that people called her the Suffragette Hornet. Parmalee gave many speeches about equality before the Vermont legislature. She argued that women paid taxes, so they should have the right to say how their tax money was spent. Her hard work paid off. In 1917, the legislature passed a law allowing women to vote in city elections. They cast their ballots the next year.

? **Want to know more?** Visit www.factsfornow .scholastic.com and enter the keyword **Vermont**.

INTO THE 20TH CENTURY

In the early 1900s, the "horseless carriage," or automobile, arrived on the American scene. In 1903, Horatio Nelson Jackson of Burlington became the first person to cross the entire United States by car. On a $50 bet, he drove from San Francisco, California, to New York City. The trip, wracked with tire blowouts and engine breakdowns, took almost two months. But Jackson proved that automobiles could be a good alternative to horses or trains for long-distance travel.

Better transportation brought a wave of tourists to Vermont. Vacation camps and resort hotels sprang up in the mountains and along rivers and lakes. Factories and mills hummed, and the state's income from manu-

Women from Vermont join others in Washington, D.C., to march for voting rights in April 1913.

facturing surpassed agriculture. Many Vermont products became useful supplies during World War I (1914–1918).

Vermont women had been fighting for woman suffrage, or the right to vote, since the 1850s. In 1880, women were permitted to vote in school board elections. Then in 1918, for the first time, women were allowed to vote in Vermont's town elections. That was two years before the 19th **Amendment**, giving women across the nation the right to vote, was added to the U.S. Constitution. As the 20th century unfolded, many distinguished Vermont women would make their mark.

WORD TO KNOW

amendment *a change to a law or legal document*

READ ABOUT

The Roaring
Twenties.....60

Depression and
Relief.......61

War and Postwar
Industries....61

The Shifting
Political
Scene.......63

Development
Versus the
Environment...65

A dairy farmer near
Fairfield, 1930s

1923 ▲
Calvin Coolidge of
Plymouth Notch
becomes the 30th
U.S. president

1927
Vermont suffers
the worst floods
in its history

1965
Redistricting gives
Vermont cities
more power in
state government

1970
Vermont limits
developments that
could harm the
environment

CHAPTER FIVE

MORE MODERN TIMES

★

IN THE EARLY 1920s, MOST VERMONT VILLAGES WERE SMALL. Few homes or businesses had telephones and people often lighted their homes with kerosene lamps. Plymouth Notch was such a village in 1923. There, on August 3 at 2:47 A.M., Vermont's Calvin Coolidge was sworn in by lamplight as the 30th U.S. president, following the death of President Warren G. Harding. Silent Cal, as he was called, served until 1929.

1984 ▶
Madeleine Kunin is elected the first female governor of Vermont

2004
Environmentalists halt construction of a highway around Burlington

2011
Tropical Storm Irene causes extensive flooding in Vermont

A family, enrolled in a New Deal Program called the Farm Security Administration, eats dinner in Bradford.

THE ROARING TWENTIES

Coolidge presided over the nation during an age known as the Roaring Twenties. It was a period of prosperity and good times. Adventurous young women turned their backs on tradition, wearing short skirts and short hairstyles and dancing the lively Charleston. George Gershwin's jazz music and F. Scott Fitzgerald's novels reflected the freewheeling lifestyles of the time. People flocked to silent films featuring romantic idol Rudolph Valentino and comedy star Charlie Chaplin. Meanwhile, gangsters made their fortunes by selling alcohol, which had been banned by the 18th Amendment to the Constitution. For much of hardworking, small-town Vermont, though, the exuberance of the Roaring Twenties was more a daydream than a reality.

DEPRESSION AND RELIEF

Vermont's worst-ever floods swept through the state in November 1927. More than 80 people lost their lives. In the Winooski River Valley, entire villages were swept away. Then, in 1929, the Great Depression began. This severe economic downturn put many Vermonters out of work as mills, factories, and other businesses closed. By 1934, nearly one-quarter of all American workers could not find jobs.

President Franklin D. Roosevelt's New Deal programs were designed to help. One program, the Civilian Conservation Corps (CCC), put unemployed people to work on projects such as building flood-control dams across **tributaries** of the Winooski River. These dams are still being used today. Another New Deal program was Social Security, which provided income for senior citizens after retirement. In 1940, 65-year-old Ida May Fuller of Brattleboro received the first Social Security check ever issued.

WAR AND POSTWAR INDUSTRIES

Although the New Deal programs brought some relief to Americans, they did not end the Depression. The nation did not emerge from the Depression until World War II began in Europe in 1939. American farms and factories began providing supplies to U.S. allies in Europe.

Although the war was initially waged among European and Asian nations, the United States became involved after Japan bombed the U.S. naval base at Pearl Harbor, Hawai'i, in 1941. People all over the state pitched in to help the war effort. Around 50,000 Vermonters served in the armed forces. Families cut down on foods such as butter and sugar because they were needed to help feed soldiers. When the government sent out a call for scrap metal to make into

WORD TO KNOW

tributaries *smaller rivers that flow into a larger river*

FAQ

Q: HOW MUCH MONEY DID IDA MAY FULLER RECEIVE FROM SOCIAL SECURITY?
A: Ida May Fuller's first payment, Social Security check number 00-000-001, was for $22.54. By the time she died at age 100, she had received $22,888.92.

A worker leads dairy cows into a barn to be milked during World War II.

SEE IT HERE!

AMERICAN PRECISION MUSEUM

The American Precision Museum is a national historic landmark in Windsor. It preserves the heritage of machine-tool manufacturing. The high-precision tools and methods developed here made modern mass production possible. You'll see early machine tools and explore the effects of the machine-tool manufacturing system on our everyday lives. Rifles, sewing machines, and typewriters are just a few of the machine-tooled items on display.

war supplies, Vermonters collected more per person than any other state. Vermont farmers produced dairy products, chicken, and beef to feed the troops. Textile mills made uniforms and wool coats. Other factories made navy ships and airplane parts.

Factories in Vermont made machine tools and high-precision instruments 24 hours a day. These instruments were so important to the war effort that the U.S. government ranked the two towns as having a high risk of being bombed by enemy planes.

As men went off to war, women took their places in the factories. Before the war, only 17 women worked in Vermont's machine-tool industry. During the war, that number rose to 528.

Tourism increased after the war. The state experienced a skiing boom as tourists flocked to the snowy slopes of the Green Mountains. Many small farms and dairies closed because they could not compete with large-scale farms operating elsewhere in the region. At the same time, large corporations opened factories in Vermont. They included International Business Machines (IBM), Husky, and General Dynamics. With new industries and more employees came a boom in home building.

In 1934, Robert Royce of Woodstock built the country's first ski tow, a machine-operated rope that pulls skiers uphill.

THE SHIFTING POLITICAL SCENE

Rural regions of Vermont had long dominated state politics. In part, this was because rural areas had greater representation in the state legislature. Voting districts were drawn based on land area instead of population. This meant that larger towns and cities had about the same influence as rural areas, despite being home to more people. In 1964, the U.S. Supreme Court ruled that this was unfair and that Vermont must **redistrict** so that each district had the same population. Finally, Vermont cities would have a fair number of votes in the state legislature.

Vermonters had supported the Republican Party since 1853. A century later, this began to change. In 1958, the people of Vermont elected Democrat William Meyer to the U.S. House of Representatives. He was the state's first Democratic congressman since 1853. In 1962, voters elected Philip Hoff as their first Democratic governor since 1853. Patrick Leahy, elected in 1974, was Vermont's first Democratic U.S. senator since the Republican Party was founded in 1854.

Around this time, women began reaching high political positions. Consuelo N. Bailey was elected Vermont's lieutenant governor in 1954. She was the first female lieutenant governor in the United States. Stella Hackel Sims

WORD TO KNOW

redistrict *to divide into new legislative districts*

MINI-BIO

CONSUELO N. BAILEY: PIONEERING POLITICIAN

Consuelo Northrop Bailey (1899–1976) was born and raised in Fairfield. As an attorney, she was the first woman to argue a case before the U.S. Supreme Court. Bailey was a real grassroots campaigner. She met with people in stores, gas stations, and churches. When she was campaigning for lieutenant governor, she even won a cow-milking contest against the other candidates! When she won the election in 1954, she became the nation's first female lieutenant governor.

? **Want to know more?** Visit www.factsfornow .scholastic.com and enter the keyword **Vermont**.

became Vermont's first female state treasurer in 1975. The next year, she was the first woman to run for governor of Vermont. As the fourth female director of the U.S. Mint (1977–1981), Sims introduced the Susan B. Anthony dollar coin. In 1984, Vermonters elected Madeleine Kunin as their governor. She was the state's first female governor, serving three terms.

Vermont's African American population began to grow after World War II, and it quadrupled between 1960 and 1990. People moved to Vermont seeking good jobs in a state famous for its inclusiveness.

Madeleine Kunin is sworn in as governor in January 1985.

Playing in the snow in Chatham

DEVELOPMENT VERSUS THE ENVIRONMENT

Tourism boomed throughout the 1960s, as tourists headed to the Green Mountains year-round. The resident population grew, too. Many people from New York and the New England states, especially Massachusetts, moved into Vermont.

All this growth had its drawbacks, though. Vermonters began to worry about the effects of growth on the environment. Concerned about how the landscape looked, Vermont banned billboards along its highways in 1968.

Vermonters have tried to protect green spaces along the state's highways.

Then, in 1970, the state passed the Environmental Control Act. It is one of the strictest environmental laws in the nation, imposing rigorous standards on housing developments, ski resorts, and other projects that could damage the land, air, or water. It also allows citizens and communities to have a voice in decisions affecting their environment. The state has also demanded that cars and factories cut down on the pollution they emit.

Today, one of Vermont's major issues is development versus the environment. The economy has grown and suburbs are spreading out far from town centers. This eliminates more and more farmland and wide-open spaces. Many farmers have sold their land.

Climate change is another concern to residents of the Green Mountain State. In the past 50 years, precipitation has increased in the state by about 20 percent. Heavy rainfall has become more frequent and intense. Since 1960, winter temperatures have risen almost 5°F (3°C). Summer temperatures have climbed by about 2°F (1°C). These changes could signal the arrival of more extreme weather patterns. In August 2011, Tropical Storm Irene slammed into the eastern United States. In Vermont, almost every river and stream flooded. Bridges were washed out and roads were badly damaged. Six Vermonters were killed and many more were left homeless. Vermont governor Peter Shumlin praised citizens' actions, saying, "We have a combination . . . of good judgment, independence, and common sense that led to a response that averted extraordinary disaster."

Charming villages such as Lyndonville still thrive throughout Vermont.

68

READ ABOUT

Population Patterns.....73

Rural Vermont.....73

Education 75

Arts and Crafts.......78

Vermont Authors 81

Sports and the Great Outdoors 82

A skier on the slopes of Stowe

CHAPTER SIX

PEOPLE

★

VERMONT MAY BE SMALL, BUT ITS TRADITIONS ARE WIDE-RANGING. Some residents preserve a New England heritage that goes back many generations. Traditional activities such as making maple syrup and gathering for county fairs are still hallmarks of Vermont life. Other residents bring new traditions from faraway lands. Rutland's annual Ethnic Festival is one of the many multicultural events that Vermonters enjoy. One and all, they find in Vermont what the state motto promises: Freedom and Unity.

Autumn means pumpkin picking for many Vermonters.

WHO LIVES IN VERMONT?

Vermonters' ancestors came from countries all over the world. Almost 95 percent of Vermonters are descended from Europeans. Only Maine has as high a percentage of people with European ancestry. Nearly one-quarter of Vermonters have French or French Canadian ancestry. Many people with French Canadian ancestry live in northern Vermont, and some still speak French at home. Many Vermonters also trace their origins to England, Germany, and Ireland. Small numbers of Vermonters are Hispanic, Asian American, or African American.

According to the 2010 census, about 2,500 Native Americans live in Vermont. The St. Francis/Sokoki Band of the Abenaki nation of Missisquoi has its headquarters in Swanton. Only in 2012 did the state of Vermont recognize it as an official Native American group.

In 1960, more than 70 percent of Vermonters had been born in the state. But by 2009, only about half of the residents had been born in Vermont. Most of the others were newcomers from other states, while some had come from other countries. Some moved to Vermont to find jobs. Others were drawn to the state because of its quiet and natural beauty.

About 5 percent of people living in Vermont are foreign-born, and Vermonters have welcomed thousands of **refugees** into their state. Many refugees have settled in the Burlington area. Some are from Somalia and Sudan in Africa, while others come from Southeast Asia, Tibet, Central America, Bosnia, and other regions.

MINI-BIO

HOMER ST. FRANCIS: REVIVING HIS PEOPLE

Homer St. Francis (1935–2001) was a descendant of Abenaki chief Grey Lock, who led raids in Massachusetts and southern Vermont in the 1700s. St. Francis himself was chief of the St. Francis/Sokoki Band of the Abenaki Nation of Missisquoi (1974–1980 and 1987–1996). Fiery and proud, he fought for Abenaki land rights. He worked hard to preserve Abenaki language and culture and to protect ancestors' remains. Eventually, thanks to his efforts, the state of Vermont formally recognized the St. Francis/Sokoki Band.

? **Want to know more?** Visit www.factsfornow .scholastic.com and enter the keyword **Vermont**.

People QuickFacts

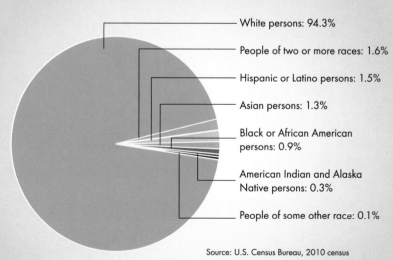

- White persons: 94.3%
- People of two or more races: 1.6%
- Hispanic or Latino persons: 1.5%
- Asian persons: 1.3%
- Black or African American persons: 0.9%
- American Indian and Alaska Native persons: 0.3%
- People of some other race: 0.1%

Source: U.S. Census Bureau, 2010 census

WORD TO KNOW

refugees *people who flee their country to escape war, disease, persecution, or other circumstances*

Where Vermonters Live

The colors on this map indicate population density throughout the state. The darker the color, the more people live there.

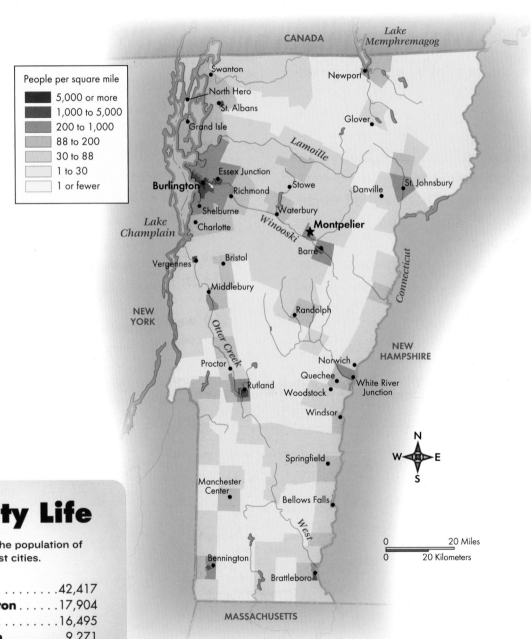

People per square mile

- 5,000 or more
- 1,000 to 5,000
- 200 to 1,000
- 88 to 200
- 30 to 88
- 1 to 30
- 1 or fewer

CANADA

Lake Memphremagog

Swanton
Newport
North Hero
St. Albans
Glover
Grand Isle
Lamoille
Essex Junction
Stowe
Danville
St. Johnsbury
Burlington
Richmond
Shelburne
Waterbury
Winooski
Montpelier
Charlotte
Barre
Lake Champlain
Vergennes
Bristol
Middlebury
Randolph
NEW YORK
Otter Creek
NEW HAMPSHIRE
Proctor
Norwich
Quechee
White River Junction
Rutland
Woodstock
Windsor
Connecticut
Springfield
Manchester Center
Bellows Falls
West
Bennington
Brattleboro
MASSACHUSETTS

N
W E
S

0   20 Miles
0   20 Kilometers

Big City Life

This list shows the population of Vermont's biggest cities.

Burlington 42,417
South Burlington 17,904
Rutland 16,495
Essex Junction 9,271
Barre 9,052

Source: U.S. Census Bureau, 2010 census

POPULATION PATTERNS

Compared to other states, Vermont has a very small population. Burlington, the state's largest city, had just over 40,000 residents in 2010. The Burlington area is the most heavily populated part of the state. Montpelier, the state capital, is home to almost 8,000 people. Vermont is also the nation's most rural state, with about 61 percent of Vermonters living outside the cities.

RURAL VERMONT

Nestled in Vermont's valleys are small towns with family-owned shops. Farmhouses and barns dot the landscape. It's said that true Vermonters have been living in the state for at least seven generations. If you're not a native Vermonter (a "woodchuck"), they are likely to call you a "flatlander." And any state south of Vermont is "down-country."

WOW

In 2010, there were 20 American cities with larger populations than the entire state of Vermont!

A view of Church Street in Burlington

Meet some typical rural Vermonters. One woman owns the village bookstore. Another is the town clerk. The postmaster knows everyone in her rural delivery area. The game warden spends his days outdoors, hoping to spot a bald eagle. And folks gather at the diner to catch up on local gossip. Compared to city life, rural life is slower and quieter.

As more newcomers arrive, however, many Vermonters worry about their rural areas. The picturesque scenes of rural Vermont are giving way to suburbs with shopping malls, movie theaters, and nationwide chain stores. Mountaintop ski areas are expanding, too.

Many citizens' groups are working to preserve Vermont's small-town character. In 1999, for example, citizens formed a grassroots organization called Vermonters for a Clean Environment. The group has successfully opposed housing developments, gas pipelines, mining operations, and other ventures that would have ruined rural landscapes.

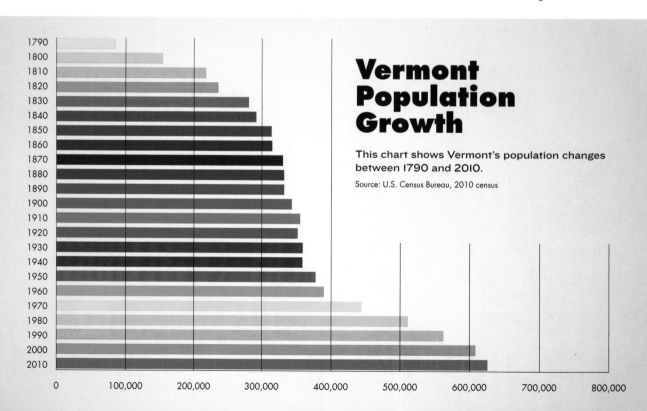

Vermont Population Growth

This chart shows Vermont's population changes between 1790 and 2010.

Source: U.S. Census Bureau, 2010 census

EDUCATION

In the 1700s, children in Vermont studied at village schools. School let out when the weather got warm so the kids could help with farmwork. Until the mid-1900s, students in some rural areas attended one-room schoolhouses. One teacher taught all grades in a single room. Today, most Vermont schoolkids attend public schools. Children must attend school from ages 6 through 16.

Vermont is home to several colleges and universities. The largest is the University of Vermont in Burlington. Middlebury College is known for its creative writing and foreign language programs. The college operates the Bread Loaf writers' workshop in Ripton. Poet Robert Frost and many other prominent writers have taught there. Marlboro College is known for its school of music, which holds the Marlboro Music Festival every summer.

The nation's first teacher-training school opened at Concord Corner in 1823.

A vendor arranges his maple syrup at a farmers' market in Montpelier.

HOW TO TALK LIKE A VERMONTER

Many Vermonters still use sayings their parents and grandparents used:

- *As stubborn as a pig on ice.*
- *As useless as a screen door on a submarine.*
- *So hungry he'd eat the north end of a southbound skunk.*
- *Slower than molasses running uphill in January.*
- *Colder than the south side of a light pole.*
- *I was so sick that I'd have to get well to die.*
- *Rain before seven, done by eleven.*
- *There'll be white blackbirds by the time he gets done.*

HOW TO EAT LIKE A VERMONTER

No food is so identified with Vermont as maple syrup. Many of the state's maple sugarhouses are small, family-owned operations deep in the woods. Favorite events at maple sugarhouses are sugar-on-snow parties during which Vermonters pour heated maple syrup onto packed snow to form a taffy-like candy. Dairy products such as milk, butter, cheese, and ice cream are Vermont favorites, too. Vermonters also enjoy other farm-based foods such as apple cider, hams, jellies, and jams.

Vermont cheese

MENU

WHAT'S ON THE MENU IN VERMONT?

★ ★ ★

Maple Products

Maple syrup, maple candy, maple sugar, maple cream, maple dressing—these are just a few of Vermont's delicious maple products.

Cheese

Vermont is famous for its delicious cheeses. Cheddar cheese is common, but Vermonters make varieties such as Gouda and blue cheese, too.

Common Crackers

The Vermont common cracker is a hard, thick cracker that's good for eating with chowder or soup. People also eat common crackers with a slab of cheddar cheese.

Ben & Jerry's Ice Cream

This local treat comes in dozens of flavors and is now sold in more than 20 countries around the world.

TRY THIS RECIPE
Maple Nut Bars

This is one of the many delicious treats you can make with Vermont maple syrup. Be sure to have an adult nearby to help.

Ingredients:

1 cup unsalted butter or margarine
1 cup sugar
2 large eggs
2 teaspoons vanilla
1 cup Vermont maple syrup
1 1/3 cups flour
1 teaspoon baking powder
2 cups oats (rolled oats, uncooked)
1 cup shredded coconut
1 cup chopped nuts

Instructions:

1. Leave the butter on the counter until it begins to soften.
2. Preheat the oven to 350°F.
3. In a large bowl, mix the butter with the sugar. Beat the eggs and stir in with the vanilla and syrup.
4. Add the rest of the ingredients and mix well.
5. Grease a 9" x 13" baking pan. Pour the mixture in and spread it around evenly.
6. Bake for 30 minutes. After the treat is cool, cut it into squares.

A pint of Ben & Jerry's ice cream

Maple syrup

The owner of a Stowe quilt shop shows off her handiwork.

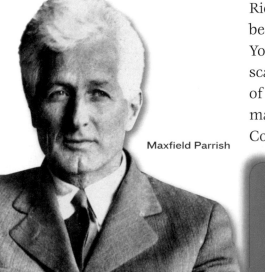

Maxfield Parrish

ARTS AND CRAFTS

Brattleboro was the hometown of two artistic brothers, Richard Morris Hunt and William Morris Hunt. Richard became an architect and designed many buildings in New York City. William became an artist who painted landscapes and portraits. Painter Maxfield Parrish spent much of his time in Windsor. He loved Vermont and painted many scenes of its landscapes. Parrish helped found the Cornish Colony, a group of painters and sculptors. It

FOLK ARTIST

Bessie Drennan (1882–1961) grew up in rural Woodbury. She wanted someone to paint a picture of her family home, but she couldn't find any artist to do it. So she attended a one-night art class in Montpelier. That was all she needed. Drennan went on to paint not only her family home, but many other charming scenes of rural Vermont life. Today, she is recognized as a gifted folk artist.

was located across the Connecticut River from Windsor, in Cornish, New Hampshire.

Many self-taught painters have lived and worked in Vermont. Their art often depicts rural scenes or farm animals and is painted with rich colors. The Shelburne Museum exhibits a large collection of folk art from the past.

Vermonters have a rich heritage of traditional arts. Wood-carvers make duck decoys, weather vanes, and many other objects. Other craftspeople produce needlework, quilts, and hand-hooked or braided rugs. Granite and marble carving, storytelling, and old-time fiddling are some other traditional arts.

Vermont's Abenaki people still practice many traditional arts. Some Abenakis weave baskets with sweetgrass and ash splints, or strips of wood from ash trees. Other Abenaki crafts include making birchbark canoes and *makuks,* which are birchbark containers used to store maple sugar and wild rice and for gathering wild fruits and berries.

Vermonters from Laos, Vietnam, and Cambodia carry on their traditional weaving, embroidery, music, and dance techniques.

MINI-BIO

JEANNE BRINK: ABENAKI BASKET MAKER

Jeanne Brink (1944–) grew up listening to tales told by her Abenaki grandmother of Thompson's Point, Vermont. Now living in Barre, Brink carries on Abenaki traditions through storytelling, music, dance, and crafts. She also helped compile an Abenaki dictionary. She is best known as a basket-making artist, creating traditional ash splint and sweetgrass basketry. She also teaches basket making to Abenaki students, hoping it will help them preserve their heritage.

? Want to know more? Visit www.factsfornow.scholastic.com and enter the keyword **Vermont**.

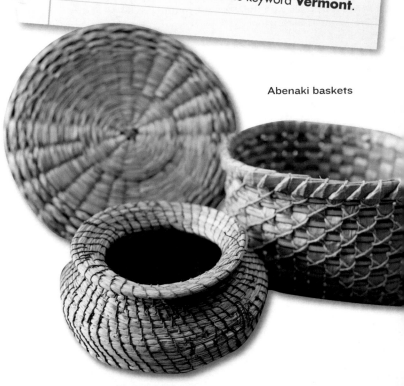

Abenaki baskets

Trey Anastasio (with guitar) of the band Phish rehearses with the Vermont Youth Orchestra in Burlington.

MUSIC

Vermont is the home to the Marlboro Music Festival, a leading classical music festival. Renowned musicians teach music students at the Marlboro festival, and both teachers and students perform there. The Vermont Symphony Orchestra is based in Burlington. It was the nation's first state-funded orchestra. Brattleboro's Vermont Theatre Company presents a Shakespeare festival every summer.

Many other kinds of music are also popular in Vermont. In the French Canadian community, there are Franco-American singers, step dancers, and fiddlers. Irish traditional musicians preserve their heritage by playing instruments such as the button accordion. Students at the University of Vermont formed the rock band Phish in 1983. The band has loyal fans in Vermont and around the world.

VERMONT AUTHORS

Many great authors have lived in Vermont. Poet Robert Frost said he moved from New Hampshire to Vermont in 1920 "to seek a better place to farm and especially grow apples." Frost's poems about New England people and places were often inspired by his experiences in Vermont. wKatherine Paterson, a Vermont children's book author, has won two Newbery Medals for best children's book of the year for *Bridge to Terabithia* and *Jacob Have I Loved*.

Author Katherine Paterson joins her son David Paterson at the world premiere of *Bridge to Terabithia* in Hollywood.

MINI-BIO

ROBERT FROST: NEW ENGLAND POET

Robert Frost (1874–1963) was a beloved poet who wrote about rural New England themes. He lived in Vermont for many years. Frost wrote his poem "Stopping by Woods on a Snowy Evening" while living in Shaftsbury. It was part of his collection *New Hampshire*, for which he won a Pulitzer Prize. In the summers, he lived in a log cabin in the Green Mountains near Ripton. He is buried in Bennington.

? **Want to know more?** Visit www.factsfornow .scholastic.com and enter the keyword **Vermont**.

WALT DISNEY PICTURES AND WALDEN ME[...]
PRESENT

BRIDGE

JOY HAKIM: STORYTELLING HISTORIAN

If you'd like to learn more about history and science, try reading the work of Joy Hakim (1931–), who was raised in Rutland. A former teacher and news reporter, Hakim is the author of the 10-volume book series for children on American history called A History of US. Written in the tone of an engaging storyteller, the books were turned into a popular public television series. A favorite among students and teachers, Hakim has also written The Story of Science. This series explores the wonders of scientific discovery from ancient civilizations to the present.

Want to know more? Visit www.factsfornow .scholastic.com and enter the keyword **Vermont**.

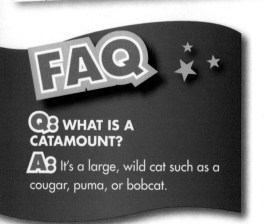

FAQ

Q: WHAT IS A CATAMOUNT?

A: It's a large, wild cat such as a cougar, puma, or bobcat.

Another writer inspired by Vermont was Dorothy Canfield Fisher. She wrote many books for both children and adults set in Vermont, including the children's book *Understood Betsy*.

SPORTS AND THE GREAT OUTDOORS

Vermont has no professional sports teams. But many Vermonters are fans of the state's college teams. Soccer, lacrosse, hockey, and basketball are major sports at the University of Vermont. Middlebury College's teams include soccer, basketball, track and field, lacrosse, hockey, and skiing.

In such a snowy state, skiing is a popular sport. Many Olympic hopefuls train on Vermont's slopes. In 1952, Vermonter Andrea Mead became the first American to win two Olympic gold medals in alpine (downhill) skiing. As of 2008, she is the only U.S. skier to have won two gold medals in a single Winter Olympics. In 1976, Bill Koch of Vermont became the first American to win an Olympic medal in cross-country skiing. At the 2006 Winter Olympics, Belmont native Hannah Teter brought home the gold medal in the women's half-pipe snowboarding event. Today, Vermonters and tourists head for ski resorts in the mountains. Popular destinations include the Stowe area, the Manchester area, and the far north.

Skiing the Green Mountains slopes

Vermonters enjoy plenty of other outdoor activities. In the winter, they go cross-country skiing, snowmobiling, snowboarding, ice-skating, and ice fishing. Fall is the time for county fairs and hikes in the woods to see the fall foliage. When it's not too cold out, people bicycle along forested trails and fish or boat on the lakes and streams. No matter what time of year it is, Vermonters find a way to enjoy the great outdoors.

The school mascot for Marlboro College is the Fighting Dead Tree!

READ ABOUT

The Capital
and the
Constitution...86

The Legislative
Branch......87

The Executive
Branch......88

The Judicial
Branch......91

Local
Government...93

Voters cast their
ballots at a 2012 town
meeting in Strafford.

CHAPTER SEVEN

GOVERNMENT

★

WHAT'S THE FIRST TUESDAY IN MARCH? In Vermont, it's Town Meeting Day! All over the state, Vermonters gather in town halls or schools. They elect officials, pass laws, and approve budgets. They vote on community issues ranging from dog licenses to road repairs. They may even discuss world issues such as climate change. At these meetings, Vermonters take part in their government directly instead of through representatives. That's why town meetings are called "the purest form of democracy."

Capitol Facts

Here are some fascinating facts about Vermont's state capitol:

Height: 136 feet (41 m)
Dome: 57 feet (17 m) high, covered with gold leaf
On top of dome: 15-foot (5 m) pine statue of Ceres, the Roman goddess of agriculture
Stories high: 2
Exterior walls: Granite from Barre
Construction dates: 1857–1859
Cost of construction: $150,000
Additions built: 1888, 1900, 1987

THE CAPITAL AND THE CONSTITUTION

Montpelier is Vermont's capital city. In terms of population, it's the smallest state capital in the country, with fewer than 10,000 residents. The stately, gold-domed capitol in downtown Montpelier is usually called the statehouse. That's where state lawmakers meet.

Vermont's constitution outlines the state's basic governing principles. Vermonters drew up their first constitution in 1777, before they attained statehood. It was a groundbreaking constitution for its time. It banned slavery and allowed voting whether a person owned property or not. New constitutions were created in 1786 and 1793. The 1793 constitution is still in effect today, after more than 200 years. Vermonters have kept the constitution up-to-date by adding amendments over the years. According to the Vermont Constitution, the state has three branches of government—legislative, executive, and judicial.

The state capitol in Montpelier

Vermont's Capital

This map shows places of interest in Montpelier, Vermont's capital city.

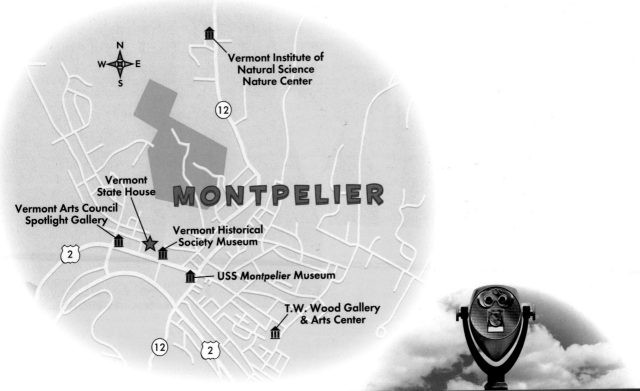

THE LEGISLATIVE BRANCH

The legislative branch of government makes state laws. Vermont's legislature is called the General Assembly. Like the U.S. Congress, it's divided into two chambers, or houses—the senate and the house of representatives.

Voters elect 30 state senators from 13 senatorial districts. Depending on a district's population, it elects one to six state senators. The house of representatives has 150 members. They come from 108 districts, where voters elect one or

SEE IT HERE!

VISIT THE VERMONT STATE HOUSE

As you enter Montpelier, you can see the golden dome of the statehouse glistening in the distance. A green lawn stretches out in front of the building, and woodsy Hubbard Park is behind it. On the portico, or front porch, is a statue of Ethan Allen, the Revolutionary War hero and founder of the Green Mountain Boys. Inside you'll see Vermont marble floors, spiral staircases, and carved-wood trim. The second floor houses the governor's office, Representatives' Hall, and the Senate Chamber. If you're there when the lawmakers are meeting, you can watch them at work.

Vermont governor Peter Shumlin outlines the state budget in 2013.

MINI-BIO

PATRICK LEAHY: VERMONT'S FIRST DEMOCRATIC SENATOR

When Patrick Leahy (1940–) was elected to the U.S. Senate in 1974, he was Vermont's youngest-ever senator and its first Democratic senator. He has served on several Senate committees, as well as being chairman of the Senate Judiciary Committee (2001–2003, 2007–). During his career, Leahy has worked to promote more openness in government and to protect citizens' phone and Internet privacy.

Want to know more? Visit www.factsfornow .scholastic.com and enter the keyword **Vermont**.

two representatives. Both senators and representatives serve two-year terms, and there is no limit on how many terms they can serve.

THE EXECUTIVE BRANCH

Vermont's governor heads the executive branch. The governor, like the assembly members, is elected to a two-year term. He or she may be reelected any number of times. Voters also elect other executive officers, including the lieutenant governor, who takes over if the governor can no longer serve; the secretary of state, who oversees elections; the attorney general, who is the top lawyer representing the state; and the auditor and treasurer, who oversee the state's finances.

The governor also appoints officials who manage areas such as health, education, transportation, housing, and the environment. Some of these appointments require approval by the state senate. Vermont's state government employs about 7,800 people throughout the state. As a result, the state government is one of Vermont's largest employers.

MINI-BIO

MADELEINE KUNIN: GOVERNOR

Born in Switzerland, Madeleine Kunin (1933–) moved with her family to the United States when she was six years old to escape persecution during World War II. She later became Vermont's first woman governor (1985–1991) and the nation's first female Jewish governor. As governor, Kunin focused on education, the environment, and women's and children's issues. She later served as U.S. ambassador to Switzerland (1996–1999).

? Want to know more? Visit www.factsfornow.scholastic.com and enter the keyword **Vermont**.

Vermont House of Representatives members take the oath of office in 2013.

Vermont State Government

EXECUTIVE BRANCH
Carries out state laws

Governor	Lieutenant Governor	Secretary of State	Attorney General	Treasurer	Auditor

Department heads of:
Agriculture
Corrections
Education
Health
Information and Innovation
Transportation
and many more

JUDICIAL BRANCH
Enforces state laws

Supreme Court

Superior Court

District Court

Family Court

Probate Court

Environmental Court

Judicial Bureau

LEGISLATIVE BRANCH
Makes and passes state laws

Senate
(30 members)

House of Representatives
(150 members)

Representing Vermont

This list shows the number of elected officials who represent Vermont, both on the state and national levels.

OFFICE	NUMBER	LENGTH OF TERM
State senators	30	2 years
State representatives	150	2 years
U.S. senators	2	6 years
U.S. representatives	1	2 years
Presidential electors	3	—

THE JUDICIAL BRANCH

Vermont's judicial branch of government is made up of judges who preside over courts. Vermont's highest court is the state supreme court, which reviews decisions made in lower courts. Vermont's supreme court consists of a chief justice, or judge, and four associate justices. They are all appointed by the governor and confirmed by the state senate.

Beneath the supreme court is the superior court, which mostly presides over civil, or noncriminal, cases. District courts hear criminal cases. Family courts handle child and family matters, and probate courts mainly deal with issues concerning a person's property after death.

VERMONTERS IN THE WHITE HOUSE

Chester A. Arthur (1829–1886) began life in a humble cabin in Fairfield, the son of an abolitionist preacher. He rose to become the vice president under President James Garfield. After Garfield was assassinated in 1881, Arthur became the 21st president. In office, he worked to reform the corrupt system of giving out government jobs as favors. This led to the creation of the civil service system. Arthur served until 1885.

Calvin Coolidge (1872–1933) was awakened in the wee hours of the morning on August 3, 1923. President Warren G. Harding had died, and Coolidge, who was vice president, would now be president. He was sworn in by lamplight at his home in Plymouth Notch, becoming the 30th president of the United States. Coolidge was the only president to be born on the Fourth of July. Because he was not very talkative, his nickname was "Silent Cal."

Vermont Counties

This map shows the 14 counties in Vermont. Montpelier, the state capital, is indicated with a star.

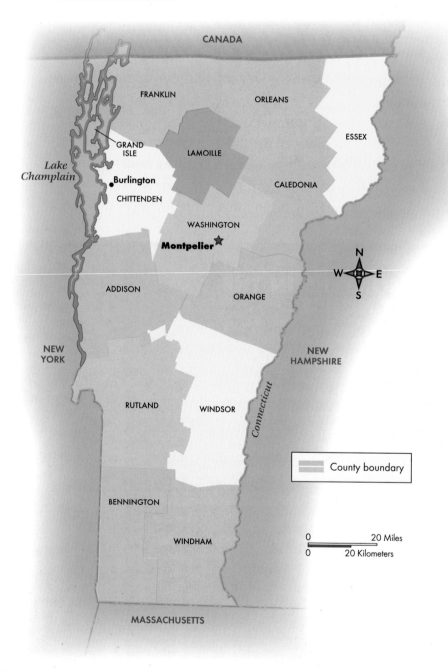

CANADA

FRANKLIN

ORLEANS

ESSEX

GRAND
ISLE

LAMOILLE

Lake
Champlain

Burlington

CALEDONIA

CHITTENDEN

WASHINGTON

Montpelier

N

W E

S

ADDISON

ORANGE

NEW
YORK

NEW
HAMPSHIRE

RUTLAND

WINDSOR

Connecticut

County boundary

BENNINGTON

WINDHAM

0   20 Miles
0   20 Kilometers

MASSACHUSETTS

LOCAL GOVERNMENT

Vermont is divided into 14 counties. In other states, county governments have many duties and functions. In Vermont, however, counties do not have much governing power. Cities and towns are the main units of local government. Vermont has nine official cities, and a mayor or city manager and a city council govern them. The state's 237 towns govern themselves through town meetings. An official town can cover a wide area. Villages are communities within towns. A village might be responsible for its own public services such as water and sewage systems.

THINK ABOUT IT!

Town Meetings: To Go or Not to Go?

Town meetings are a long-standing tradition in Vermont. Yet, on average, only about 20 percent of the voters go to the meetings. Why do people choose to attend or not attend?

PRO

The town meeting is "one of the few places where people still can make a difference."
—Margaret Vittum, Hubbardton town clerk

"We take great pride in having our say not just in how things are run in our towns, but also on bigger issues like war and peace."
—Randolph T. Holhut, Dummerston

CON

A town meeting can be "a long day of sitting on a hard chair listening to people argue."
—Frank Bryan, Professor Emeritus of Political Science, University of Vermont

"Some people don't care to get involved in participatory democracy. Others just find town meetings, well, boring."
—John Dillon, Vermont Public Radio

State Flag

The original Vermont state flag was designed in October 1803. Its design featured 17 stripes and stars, representing the 17 states of the Union at that time. The problem with this design was that the American flag and Vermont flag looked too similar. It wasn't until 1837 that the Vermont legislature decided to design a new flag. This flag was very similar to the first design, however. The current flag design was adopted in 1923.

State Seal

The General Assembly of Vermont adopted the first state seal in 1779. Since its adoption, the state seal has changed several times. In 1937, a final design for the state seal was approved, and it is still in use today. In the center of the seal is a pine tree, along with a depiction of Vermont's forests. The seal also features a cow and bundles of wheat, which represent the state's agricultural strength. The Vermont state motto, "Freedom & Unity," is displayed along the bottom of the seal.

96

READ ABOUT

Service
Industries 98

Made in
Vermont 99

Agriculture . . 101

Mining 102

Harvesting lettuce
in Shaftsbury

CHAPTER EIGHT

ECONOMY

★

MAPLE SYRUP AND COMPUTER CHIPS, TEDDY BEARS AND AIRPLANE PARTS, ICE CREAM AND BIG BLOCKS OF STONE. These are just a few of the products proudly made in Vermont. But Vermonters do many kinds of work besides making products. Many Vermonters help keep the state's economy running by doing things for other people. From the man who delivers pizza to the woman who teaches a math class, they provide services everyone needs.

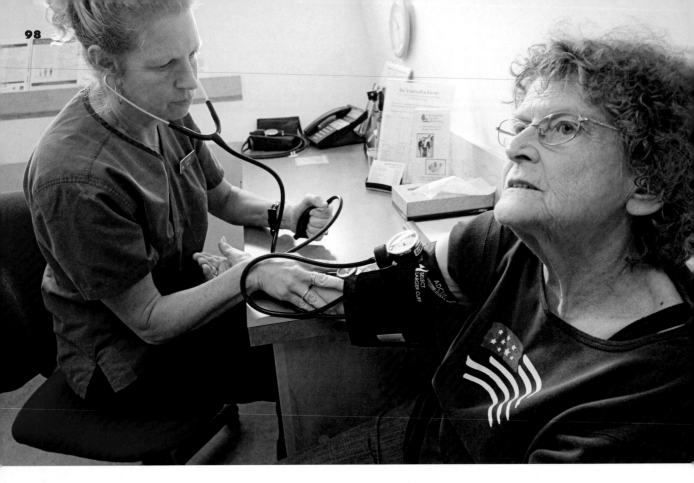

A nurse in Plainfield measures a
patient's blood pressure.

SERVICE INDUSTRIES

Service industries employ the most people and bring the
most income into Vermont. Service workers are people
who do things for other people, instead of producing
goods such as granite, apples, or machines. Some service
workers help customers in stores, and others drive delivery trucks. Lawyers, bank tellers, car salespeople, doc-
tors, and teachers all work in service industries.

Tourism puts thousands of people to work in Vermont.
This includes people who work at ski lodges, hotel and
restaurant workers, museum guides, and people who rent
snowmobiles. Real estate agents are busy in Vermont, too.
They buy, sell, and rent homes. Some of their customers
are vacationers, while others are moving into Vermont to
live and work.

Top Products

Agriculture Dairy products, beef cattle, hay, honey, maple syrup, nursery and greenhouse products, corn, apples, potatoes

Manufacturing Electrical and electronic equipment, metal products, food products, machinery

Mining Granite, marble, crushed stone (limestone), sand and gravel, talc

Lake Champlain chocolates

Government employees are also service workers. Many of them are employed in the state's public schools as teachers, secretaries, cafeteria workers, or janitors. Others may work for public hospitals, libraries, driver license bureaus, or parks.

MADE IN VERMONT

Computer chips, tools, ice cream, machines, and glass— these are just a few of Vermont's factory goods. Electrical and electronic equipment are the state's top manufactured products. Food products are also leading manufactured goods. Cheese is the top product, along with other dairy foods such as butter and ice cream. Many rural towns have their own cheese factories that make cheese with milk from local dairy farms. Vermont brands such as Cabot Cheese and the Vermont Butter & Cheese Company are known nationwide. Ben & Jerry's ice cream factory is located in Waterbury. Ice cream lovers stop by to tour the factory and sample the latest flavors. Chocolate is another delicious Vermont food. Lake Champlain Chocolates in Burlington makes more than 1 million pounds (454,000 kilograms) of chocolate every year!

ELISHA OTIS: ELEVATOR MAN

Walk into an elevator, and you're likely to see the name Otis somewhere. That's because Elisha Graves Otis (1811–1861) invented the safety elevator—one that won't fall if the cables break. Born and raised on a farm near Halifax, Otis was always a bit sickly. He worked as a carpenter and then taught himself mechanics. He developed his elevator while trying to figure out how to hoist heavy machines to a building's upper floors. His Otis Elevator Company became the world's largest elevator company.

? **Want to know more?** Visit www.factsfornow .scholastic.com and enter the keyword **Vermont**.

What Do Vermonters Do?

This color-coded chart shows what industries Vermonters work in.

Metal products are valuable factory goods in Vermont. They include guns, tools, metal construction supplies, and parts for aircraft engines.

Some of the trees grown in Vermont are used to make furniture, wooden bowls, paper, and cardboard. Glass, concrete, and plastics are some of Vermont's other factory goods. And let's not forget teddy bears. Workers at the Vermont Teddy Bear Company in Shelburne make and stuff teddy bears

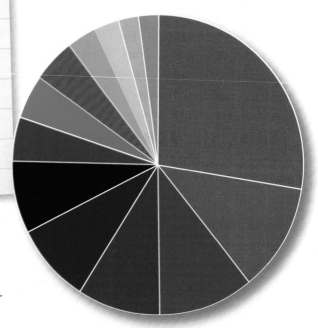

27.6% Educational services, and health care and social assistance 90,505

11.7% Retail trade 38,481

10.6% Manufacturing 34,773

9.2% Arts, entertainment, and recreation, and accommodation and food services 30,057

8.6% Professional, scientific, and management, and administrative and waste management services 28,287

7.6% Construction 24,754

4.8% Finance and insurance, and real estate and rental and leasing 15,878

4.8% Public administration 15,575

4.5% Other services, except public administration 14,679

3.4% Transportation and warehousing, and utilities 11,086

2.7% Agriculture, forestry, fishing and hunting, and mining 8,888

2.4% Wholesale trade 7,834

2.0% Information 6,702

Source: U.S. Census Bureau, 2010 census

Cattle grazing on a Vermont farm

by hand. You can watch them at work and even make your own bear!

AGRICULTURE

Dairy cows, calmly grazing and munching, are a common sight in rural Vermont. They and their milk are the basis of the state's dairy industry. Raising dairy cows is Vermont's leading agricultural activity. Many farmers raise beef cattle and calves, too. Hogs, sheep, and chickens are also valuable farm animals.

The cattle need food, and hay provides it. Hay is Vermont's top crop. In fact, Vermont produces more hay, milk, and dairy cattle than any other New England state. Apples are the leading fruit grown in the state, and sweet corn is the top vegetable. Vermonters also raise greenhouse and nursery products such as Christmas trees.

It can take up to 40 gallons
(151 liters) of maple sap to make
1 gallon (4 l) of maple syrup!

SEE IT HERE!

ROCK OF AGES

The Rock of Ages granite quarry is in Barre, the capital of Vermont's granite industry. There you'll watch workers cut giant granite blocks out of Millstone Hill. You'll see monster cranes lift blocks that weigh several tons. At the world's largest stone-finishing plant, craftspeople saw, polish, and carve the blocks of stone. You'll even learn how to sandblast and create your own granite souvenir.

Rock of Ages quarried the world's biggest block of stone in 1913. It measured 200 feet (61 m) long, 80 feet (24 m) wide, and 24 feet (7 m) thick, and it weighed about 32,500 tons!

Vermont is the nation's top producer of maple syrup and maple sugar. Maple season begins in early spring. People go into the sugar bush, or maple tree groves, make holes in the trunks to tap the sap, and collect it in buckets. In the sugarhouse, they boil the sap to reduce it to thick, sweet syrup.

MINING

Vermont has three top mineral products. One of them is dimension stone. That's stone quarried in big blocks or slabs. It's then cut, trimmed into shape, and polished. The stone is used for monuments, kitchen countertops, walls of buildings, and many other structures. Most of Vermont's dimension stone is granite, while some is marble. The Rock of Ages granite quarry in the Barre area is the main source of granite. Most of the marble comes from the Champlain Valley and the Vermont Valley.

Another leading mineral product is crushed stone. Most of that is limestone, which is used in building roads and protecting shorelines. Crushed marble, or calcium carbonate, may not seem like something you could eat. But it's used in toothpaste, gum, and many foods that contain calcium. Other top mineral products are sand and gravel. Combined, they're made into concrete and asphalt and sprinkled on snowy and icy roads.

Vermont ranks among the top three states in mining talc. This soft mineral is found in southern Vermont. Ground-up talc is used as an additive in cosmetics, plastics, paper, rubber, paint, roofing, and flooring. Slate mining is a smaller industry today than it was in the past. Today, slate quarries operate near the Vermont–New York border around Fair Haven.

Major Agricultural and Mining Products

This map shows where Vermont's major agricultural and mining products come from. See a cow? That means cattle are raised there.

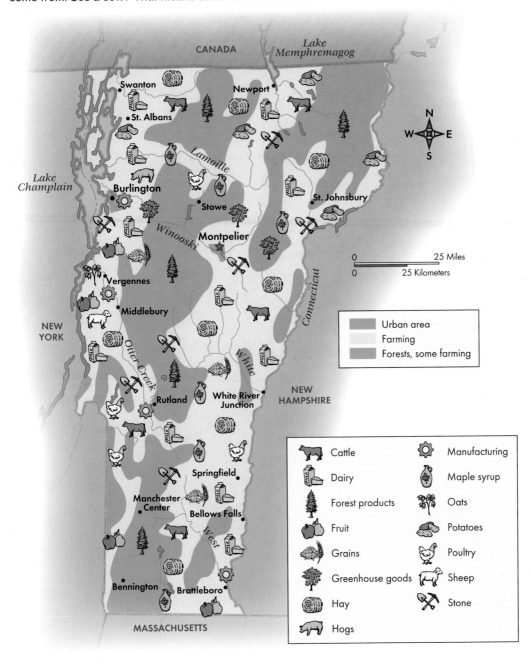

Legend:

- Urban area
- Farming
- Forests, some farming

Symbol	Product	Symbol	Product
Cattle	Cattle	Manufacturing	Manufacturing
Dairy	Dairy	Maple syrup	Maple syrup
Forest products	Forest products	Oats	Oats
Fruit	Fruit	Potatoes	Potatoes
Grains	Grains	Poultry	Poultry
Greenhouse goods	Greenhouse goods	Sheep	Sheep
Hay	Hay	Stone	Stone
Hogs	Hogs		

Map labels: CANADA, Lake Memphremagog, Swanton, Newport, St. Albans, Lamoille, Lake Champlain, Burlington, Stowe, St. Johnsbury, Winooski, Montpelier, Vergennes, Middlebury, NEW YORK, Otter Creek, White, Rutland, White River Junction, NEW HAMPSHIRE, Connecticut, Springfield, Manchester Center, Bellows Falls, West, Bennington, Brattleboro, MASSACHUSETTS

Scale: 0 — 25 Miles; 0 — 25 Kilometers

CANADA

*Lake
Memphremagog*

Swanton

Jay

Newport

Derby Line

North Hero

89

St. Albans

Brownington

Island Pond

Grand Isle

Glover

*Lake
Champlain*

Lamoille

West Burke

Burke Hollow

91

East Burke

Essex Junction

Stowe

Danville

St. Johnsbury

Burlington

Richmond

Waterbury

93

Shelburne

Winooski

Montpelier

Charlotte

Barre

N

Vergennes

Bristol

W   E

Weybridge

Geographic
Center of
Vermont

S

Addison

Middlebury

**NEW
HAMPSHIRE**

Randolph

89

Otter Creek

Norwich

91

Proctor

White River
Junction

**NEW
YORK**

Quechee

Rutland

Woodstock

Connecticut

Plymouth

Windsor

Springfield

89 ─── Interstate highway

Manchester
Center

West

Bellows Falls

0   20 Miles

91

0   20 Kilometers

Bennington

Marlboro

Stamford

Brattleboro

MASSACHUSETTS

CHAPTER NINE

TRAVEL GUIDE

★

Travel through Vermont to discover great beauty and historic treasures. You'll hike along nature trails, learn about early cultures, and ski through snowy woods. Friendly Vermonters are happy to show you how they make maple syrup, cheese, ice cream, teddy bears, and music boxes. Wherever you go in Vermont, you'll find a spot to explore!

← Follow along with this travel map. We'll begin our trip in Derby Line and go all the way down to Bennington.

NORTHEAST KINGDOM

THINGS TO DO: Go skiing or snowmobiling, wander through a corn maze, or learn about the stars.

Derby Line

★ **Haskell Opera House:** You'll have an international experience in this elegant old opera house. It sits right on Vermont's border with Canada. When you watch a show, you're sitting in the United States while the performers onstage are in Canada!

Jay

★ **Jay Peak Aerial Tram:** Take to the sky on this ride to the top of Jay Peak. From the summit, you'll enjoy incredible views. Ski down the mountain in the winter, or enjoy a mountaintop picnic in the summer.

Island Pond

★ **Snowmobiling:** This town calls itself the snowmobile capital of Vermont. Miles of trails wind through the meadows and woods. In the winter, you can join in the snowmobile races on Island Pond Lake.

Bread and Puppet Museum

Glover

★ **Bread and Puppet Museum:** Here you can see hundreds of puppets and masks made for the Bread and Puppet Theater. During the summer, the museum hosts workshops on puppet making and other crafts.

Brownington

★ **Old Stone House Museum:** African American minister Alexander Twilight built this four-story granite building in 1836 as a dormitory for students at the Orleans County Grammar School, where he served as principal. Nearby are the three-room house and the larger, two-story home where Twilight and his family lived.

Burke

★ **Burke Mountain:** If you like skiing, this is the place for you. Many Olympic skiers got their training on these slopes. Whether you're a beginner or an expert, you'll find ski trails that match your skills on Burke Mountain.

Saint Johnsbury

★ **Fairbanks Museum & Planetarium:** Exhibits at this museum highlight the region's natural resources, climate, culture, and human settlement patterns. The museum also houses Vermont's only public planetarium, where you can see a sky show and learn about space travel and the solar system.

★ **Maple Grove Farms:** Be sure to sample some delicious maple candies while you're here. Then stroll over to the Sugar House Museum to get the full story of the sugaring process.

★ **Dog Mountain:** This dog-lover's complex features a Dog Chapel, where both dogs and people are welcome. The Showhouse is full of dog-themed artwork and furniture by artist Stephen Huneck, and the gift shop offers dog art, cards, books, rugs, sculptures, and much more.

North Danville

★ **Great Vermont Corn Maze:** Come by from August through October to wind your way through 10 acres (4 ha) of trails through towering rows of corn. Creep through "gopher tunnels," or walk above the maze on bridges. It takes from 40 minutes to over two hours to get through the maze, but there's an emergency exit if you must get out!

Dog Chapel on Dog Mountain

CHAMPLAIN VALLEY

THINGS TO DO: Explore Abenaki culture, discover how bees make wax, visit a Morgan horse stable, make your own teddy bear, or learn about shipwrecks.

Swanton

★ **Abenaki Tribal Museum:** This museum is located next to the Abenaki tribal headquarters. Here you'll get a fascinating glimpse into the history and culture of the Abenaki people.

Saint Albans

★ **Vermont Maple Festival:** This festival takes place on the last full weekend in April. Enjoy pancake breakfasts, New England craft exhibits, maple candy-making demonstrations, pony rides, carnival rides, and a huge parade.

Lake Champlain

★ **Underwater shipwrecks:** If you're a scuba diver, you can explore several shipwrecks in Vermont's underwater historic sites. Among the sunken vessels are a horse ferry, a coal barge, cargo ships, military boats, and passenger ships.

A ferry on Lake Champlain

Grand Isle

★ **Lake Champlain ferries:** Catch a ferryboat here for a ride across Lake Champlain to New York State and back. You can begin ferry crossings from Burlington and Charlotte, too.

Charlotte

★ **Vermont Wildflower Farm:** Stroll along the winding pathways through 6 acres (2.4 ha) of wildflowers that bloom each season.

North Hero

★ **Herrmann's Royal Lipizzan Stallions:** Every summer, these magnificent white horses tour and put on shows. You can also visit them in their stables during the winter.

Burlington

★ **Church Street Marketplace:** This historic marketplace is in the heart of downtown Burlington. It features more than 130 shops and restaurants and hosts events and festivals throughout the year.

Richmond

★ **Old Round Church:** Built in the early 1800s, this historic church is actually 16-sided. Until 1973, Richmond's town meetings were held here, as were church services for five religions.

Shelburne Farms

Shelburne

★ **Shelburne Farms:** At this 1,400-acre (567 ha) working farm, you can walk the trails or hop aboard a truck-drawn shuttle. You'll visit the farm animals and take part in daily farm activities, from grooming a horse to gathering eggs. You can also watch workers make cheddar cheese.

★ **Shelburne Museum:** This sprawling museum is built like an early New England village, with more than 30 historic buildings. Walk through the village and see carriages, textiles, toys, dolls, paintings, and many other artifacts of early American life. You'll also see the *Ticonderoga*, a side-wheel steamship.

★ **Vermont Teddy Bear Company:** Take a tour of this teddy bear factory to see how cuddly, handmade bears are put together. You can even make your own teddy bear, stuff it, and name it.

Vergennes

★ **Vergennes Opera House:**
Originally built in 1897, this opera
house has been fully restored.
Today, visitors can view plays,
concerts, and a variety of other
performances.

★ **Lake Champlain Maritime
Museum:** Head down to Basin
Harbor, where more than a dozen
buildings house exhibits on Lake
Champlain's history. You'll see
antique boats, shipwreck exhibits,
and a working blacksmith shop. You
can also climb aboard a full-sized
Revolutionary War gunboat.

Addison

★ **Chimney Point State Historic
Site:** Humans have lived at this site
for 9,000 years. Visit the site to see
ancient artifacts and learn about the
region's Native American, French
colonial, and early American people.

Bristol

★ **Vermont HoneyLights:** Discover
the magic of beeswax and its amaz-
ing journey from bee to candle.
You'll learn how bees use a "waggle
dance" to tell other bees where to
find nectar and find out how many
flowers a bee must visit to make 1
pound (0.5 kg) of beeswax. You can
also watch artists using beeswax
to create hand-rolled or poured
candles.

Middlebury

★ **Vermont Soap Factory Outlet and
Soap Museum:** Watch people make
soap using a 200-year-old technique.
They mix a batch in a big tub, cook
and stir it, and pour the liquid soap
into molds. You'll also see hand-
cranked washing machines and
other old-fashioned washing gadgets.

Weybridge

★ **Morgan Horse Farm:** The
University of Vermont operates this
farm for Morgan horses. Watch these
beautiful horses on acres of green
pastureland, tour the stables, and
see a video to learn about Morgans.

Morgan Horse Farm

CENTRAL VERMONT

THINGS TO DO: See how ice cream and maple syrup are made, explore centuries of Vermont history, and have an up-close encounter with birds of prey.

Stowe

★ **Mount Mansfield:** Drive or hike up the highest mountain in Vermont. From the east, it looks like the profile of a human face. See if you can pick out the points named the Forehead, Adam's Apple, Nose, and Chin!

★ **Smugglers' Notch:** People used to sneak illegal goods through this gap in the Green Mountains. Today, you can enjoy skiing and snowboarding in the area.

★ **Stowe Winter Carnival:** This January festival features a spectacular ice carving contest as well as ski races, snow golf, a kids' carnival, and the Village Night Block Party.

Montpelier

★ **Vermont State House:** Tour the state capitol and see where the state senators and representatives meet.

Outside the Ben & Jerry's Factory

Waterbury

★ **Ben & Jerry's Factory Tour:** Enjoy a "moo-vie" in the Cow over the Moon Theater. You'll learn how two childhood friends, Ben Cohen and Jerry Greenfield, started their company. Watch the ice cream–making process and sample the flavor of the day.

SEE IT HERE!

VERMONT HISTORY MUSEUM

Visit this museum in Montpelier, and you'll experience Vermont's history with all your senses. You can smell the scents from an old general store, touch a telegraph, sit in a World War II living room, watch a movie about the Great Flood of 1927, or listen to the voices of 20th-century Vermonters. The centerpiece is the Vermont Historical Society's exhibit Freedom and Unity: One Ideal, Many Stories.

Randolph

★ **Porter Music Box Company:** Long before the electronic age, people listened to music boxes. This is the only factory in the world that still makes large, tabletop-sized music boxes.

Plymouth

★ **Plymouth Notch Historic District:** Here you can tour President Calvin Coolidge's birthplace, the home where he took his oath of office, and the cemetery where he is buried. Other buildings in the historic district include a general store and a visitors' center.

Calvin Coolidge's birthplace

Proctor

★ **Vermont Marble Museum:** Here you'll learn the history of Vermont's marble industry. Through hands-on exhibits, you'll see how activity within the earth creates marble. Browse the world's largest collection of marble types, visit the theater, or try carving marble with the resident sculptor.

Pittsford

★ **New England Maple Museum:** Take a trip through Vermont's maple industry in the sugarhouse. You'll watch the boiling process and learn about maple sugaring from sap to syrup. Be sure to stop by the tasting counter, too.

SEE IT HERE!

MARSH-BILLINGS-ROCKEFELLER NATIONAL HISTORICAL PARK

This estate in Woodstock was the home of George Perkins Marsh, one of the nation's first environmentalists. Tour the mansion with its extensive art collection. Then learn about the history of conservation as you walk through the 550-acre (223 ha) forest. You'll pass sugar maples, 400-year-old hemlock trees, covered bridges, and rambling stone walls.

Woodstock

★ **Billings Farm & Museum:** This museum of rural Vermont life is a working dairy farm, featuring interactive activities and historical exhibits. Pet the farm animals and watch daily farm activities such as the afternoon cow milking.

★ **Sugarbush Farm:** Visit this working maple syrup and cheese farm to learn how maple syrup is made—and then taste it! Watch cheese being hand cut, waxed, and packaged. Then visit the farm animals and walk the maple trail through the woods.

Quechee

★ **Quechee Gorge:** This deep canyon is called Vermont's Grand Canyon. You'll see beautiful views as you gaze out from the bridge 163 feet (50 m) above the Ottauquechee River. Enjoy nature along the hiking trails and have a picnic overlooking the waterfalls.

★ **Quechee Gorge Village:** Browse hundreds of shops—where you can buy local products such as cheese, handcrafts, and pewter—as well as a country store and a blacksmith shop. You might also want to visit the Vermont Toy and Train Museum or take a train or carousel ride.

Billings Farm and Museum

★ **Vermont Institute of Natural Science (VINS) Nature Center:** Here you can see live birds of prey such as owls, eagles, vultures, hawks, and falcons. Species include bald and golden eagles, snowy owls, peregrine falcons, and red-tailed hawks. Daily programs demonstrate the birds' behavior and flight patterns.

Norwich

★ **Montshire Museum of Science:** Inside this museum, you'll see live animals, aquariums, and exhibits on space, nature, and technology. Outside, you can explore nature trails and visit the science park and learning center.

SOUTHERN VERMONT

THINGS TO DO: Hike through the wilderness, ride a train through the mountains, feed baby fish, or see one of the world's tallest battle monuments.

Springfield

★ **Stellafane Observatory National Historic Landmark:** First, climb to the top of Breezy Hill to visit the pink clubhouse of the Springfield Telescope Makers. They are an amateur group of astronomers and telescope makers. Then check out the Porter Turret Telescope. It's designed like the telescope invented by British scientist Isaac Newton in the 1600s.

★ **Eureka Schoolhouse:** Built from 1785 to 1790, this is Vermont's oldest surviving one-room schoolhouse. Classes were held there until 1900. Students in all grades had classes in the same room.

Manchester Center

★ **Green Mountain National Forest, Manchester Ranger Station:** This information center is a great place to begin your adventures in Green Mountain National Forest. Explore the wilderness and enjoy hiking, picnicking, berry picking, bird-watch-

ing, fishing, hunting, cross-country skiing, and snowmobiling.

Windsor

★ **American Precision Museum:** At this museum, you can see early machine tools and explore the effects of machine-tool manufacturing on our everyday lives.

★ **Old Constitution House:** This is where Vermonters adopted their first constitution. Built in 1772, this two-story house used to be a tavern.

★ **Mt. Ascutney State Park:** Established in 1935, this park covers around 2,000 acres (809 ha) of beautiful forestland. Visitors can hike along the park's trails for incredible views and spend the night at a variety of camp sites.

Eureka Schoolhouse

Hiking the Long Trail

Stamford

★ **The Long Trail:** Would you like to hike the entire length of Vermont? This hiking trail runs along the Green Mountains, with beautiful mountain scenery every step of the way. It begins near Stamford at the Massachusetts border and extends 273 miles (439 km) north all the way to the Canadian border.

Bellows Falls

★ **Green Mountain Railroad:** Hop aboard this train for a scenic trip through the mountains.

Marlboro

★ **Southern Vermont Natural History Museum:** Here you'll see hundreds of birds and mammals mounted in displays showing their natural habitat. You'll see reptiles and amphibians in the Vermont wetland exhibit, and live hawks, owls, and other birds of prey in the raptor center.

Bennington

★ **Bennington Battle Monument:** This limestone tower is one of the world's tallest battle monuments, rising 306 feet (93 m) high. It honors the colonists' 1777 victory over the British in the Battle of Bennington during the American Revolution.

★ **Bennington Fish Culture Station:** Here fish are grown from tiny eggs. When they are adults, they are released into Vermont's lakes and streams. You might even get to feed the fish or see animals such as great blue herons, ospreys, otters, or minks. This is one of Vermont's five fish hatcheries. Others are in Salisbury, Roxbury, Newark, and Grand Isle.

WRITING PROJECTS

Check out these ideas for creating a campaign brochure and writing you-are-there narratives. Or research the lives of famous Vermonters.

118

ART PROJECTS

You can illustrate the state song, create a dazzling PowerPoint presentation, or learn about the state quarter and design your own.

119

TIMELINE

What happened when? This timeline highlights important events in the state's history—and shows what was happening throughout the United States at the same time.

122

FAST FACTS

Use this section to find fascinating facts about state symbols, land area and population statistics, weather, sports teams, and much more.

126

GLOSSARY

Remember the Words to Know from the chapters in this book? They're all collected here.

125

SCIENCE, TECHNOLOGY, & MATH PROJECTS

Make weather maps, graph population statistics, and research endangered species that live in the state.

120

PRIMARY VS. SECONDARY SOURCES

121

So what are primary and secondary sources? And what's the diff? This section explains all that and where you can find them.

BIOGRAPHICAL DICTIONARY

133

This at-a-glance guide highlights some of the state's most important and influential people. Visit this section and read about their contributions to the state, the country, and the world.

RESOURCES

Books, Web sites, DVDs, and more. Take a look at these additional sources for information about the state.

138

WRITING PROJECTS

Write a Memoir, Journal, or Editorial for Your School Newspaper!

Picture Yourself . . .

★ In an Abenaki sugar camp. It's early spring, and snow is still on the ground. The grown-ups have been watching the moon and the weather. They know it's time to go sugaring. What would life be like living in the sugar camp?
   SEE: Chapter Two, page 30.

★ Living in the Vermont wilderness in the 1700s. Snow blankets the landscape, and chill winds whistle around the log cabin. Stew is boiling in a big, iron kettle over the fireplace. As you glance around the cabin, almost everything you see reminds you of your work in the spring and summer. Describe some of the hardships of living in the wilds of Vermont.
   SEE: Chapter Three, pages 41–43.

Create an Election Brochure or Web Site!

Run for office! Throughout this book, you've read about some of the issues that concern Vermont today. As a candidate for governor of Vermont, create a campaign brochure or Web site.

★ Explain how you meet the qualifications to be governor of Vermont.

★ Talk about the three or four major issues you'll focus on if you're elected.

★ Remember, you'll be responsible for Vermont's budget. How would you spend the taxpayers' money?
   SEE: Chapter Seven, pages 88–89.

Create an interview script with a famous person from Vermont!

★ Research various Vermonters, such as Ethan Allen, Lemuel Haynes, Consuelo N. Bailey, Robert Frost, Katherine Paterson, and many others.

★ Based on your research, pick one person you would most like to talk with.

★ Write a script of the interview. What questions would you ask? How would this person answer? Create a question-and-answer format. You may want to supplement this writing project with a voice-recording dramatization of the interview.
   SEE: Chapters Three, Four, Five, and Six, pages 39, 53, 64, 81, and the Biographical Dictionary, pages 133–137.

ART PROJECTS

Create a PowerPoint Presentation or Visitors' Guide

Welcome to Vermont!

Vermont's a great place to visit and to live! From its natural beauty to its historical sites, there's plenty to see and do. In your PowerPoint presentation or brochure, highlight 10 to 15 of Vermont's fascinating landmarks. Be sure to include:

★ a map of the state showing where these sites are located

★ photos, illustrations, Web links, natural history facts, geographic stats, climate and weather, plants and wildlife, and recent discoveries

SEE: Chapter Nine, pages 104–115, and Fast Facts, pages 126–127.

Illustrate the Lyrics to the Vermont State Song

("These Green Mountains")

Use markers, paints, photos, collages, colored pencils, or computer graphics to illustrate the lyrics to "These Green Mountains." Turn your illustrations into a picture book, or scan them into PowerPoint and add music.

SEE: The lyrics to "These Green Mountains" on page 128.

Research Vermont's State Quarter

From 1999 to 2008, the U.S. Mint introduced new quarters commemorating each of the 50 states in the order that they were admitted to the Union. Each state's quarter features a unique design on its reverse, or back.

★ Research the significance of the image. Who designed the quarter? Who chose the final design?

★ Design your own Vermont quarter. What images would you choose for the reverse?

★ Make a poster showing the Vermont quarter and label each image.

GO TO: www.factsfornow.scholastic.com. Enter the keyword **Vermont** and look for the link to the Vermont quarter.

SCIENCE, TECHNOLOGY, ENGINEERING, & MATH PROJECTS

Graph Population Statistics!

★ Compare population statistics (such as ethnic background, birth, death, and literacy rates) in Vermont counties or major cities.

★ In your graph or chart, look at population density and write sentences describing what the population statistics show; graph one set of population statistics and write a paragraph explaining what the graphs reveal.

SEE: Chapter Six, pages 70–74.

Create a Weather Map of Vermont!

Use your knowledge of Vermont's geography to research and identify conditions that result in specific weather events. What is it about the geography of Vermont that makes it vulnerable to heavy snow? Create a weather map or poster that shows the weather patterns over the state. Include a caption explaining the technology used to measure weather phenomena and provide data.

SEE: Chapter One, pages 18–19.

Osprey

Track Endangered Species

Using your knowledge of Vermont's wildlife, research which animals and plants are endangered or threatened.

★ Find out what the state is doing to protect these species.

★ Chart known populations of the animals and plants, and report on changes in certain geographic areas.

SEE: Chapter One, page 22.

PRIMARY VS. SECONDARY SOURCES

What's the Diff?

Your teacher may require at least one or two primary sources and one or two secondary sources for your assignment. So, what's the difference between the two?

★ **Primary sources are original.** You are reading the actual words of someone's diary, journal, letter, autobiography, or interview. Primary sources can also be photographs, maps, prints, cartoons, news/film footage, posters, first-person newspaper articles, drawings, musical scores, and recordings.

  By the way, when you conduct a survey, interview someone, shoot a video, or take photographs to include in a project, you are creating primary sources!

★ **Secondary sources are what you find in encyclopedias, textbooks, articles, biographies, and almanacs.** These are written by a person or group of people who tell about something that happened to someone else. Secondary sources also recount what another person said or did. This book is an example of a secondary source.

Now that you know what primary sources are—where can you find them?

★ **Your school or local library:** Check the library catalog for collections of original writings, government documents, musical scores, and so on. Some of this material may be stored on microfilm.

★ **Historical societies:** These organizations keep historical documents, photographs, and other materials. Staff members can help you find what you are looking for. History museums are also great places to see primary sources firsthand.

★ **The Internet:** There are lots of sites that have primary sources you can download and use in a project or assignment.

TIMELINE

U.S. Events

9000 BCE

6000 BCE

4000 BCE

1000 BCE

1600 CE

1607
The first permanent English settlement in North America is established at Jamestown.

1620
Pilgrims found Plymouth Colony, the second permanent English settlement.

1682
René-Robert Cavelier, Sieur de La Salle, claims more than 1 million square miles (2.6 million sq km) of territory in the Mississippi River basin for France, naming it Louisiana.

1700

1754–63
England and France fight over North American colonial lands in the French and Indian War. By the end of the war, France has ceded all of its land west of the Mississippi to Spain and its Canadian territories to England.

Vermont Events

c. 9000 BCE
Paleo-Indians begin hunting in today's Vermont.

c. 6000 BCE
The Archaic culture develops.

c. 4000 BCE
The climate warms and the population grows.

c. 1000 BCE
People begin hunting with bows and arrows and making clay pottery.

c. 1600 CE
About 6,000 Abenakis live in Vermont.

1609
French explorer Samuel de Champlain is the first European to reach Vermont.

1666
The French build Fort Sainte Anne on Isle La Motte.

1724
The British build Fort Dummer, the first permanent white settlement in Vermont, near today's Brattleboro.

1763
Great Britain gains control of Vermont after the French and Indian War.

c. 1770
Ethan Allen organizes the Green Mountain Boys to drive New York settlers out of Vermont.

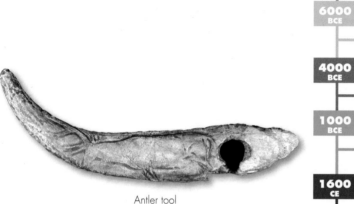

Antler tool

U.S. Events

1776
Thirteen American colonies declare their independence from Great Britain.

1787
The U.S. Constitution is written.

1803
The Louisiana Purchase almost doubles the size of the United States.

1812–15
The United States and Great Britain fight the War of 1812.

John Deere

1846–48
The United States fights a war with Mexico over western territories in the Mexican War.

1917–18
The United States engages in World War I.

1920
The Nineteenth Amendment to the U.S. Constitution grants women the right to vote.

Vermont Events

1775
The Green Mountain Boys capture Fort Ticonderoga from the British in the Revolutionary War.

1777
Vermont declares itself an independent republic and adopts its first constitution, which outlaws slavery.

1791
Vermont becomes the 14th U.S. state on March 4.

1800

1805
Montpelier is chosen as the state capital.

c. 1814
Barre's first granite quarry opens.

1820
Vermont's legislature passes a resolution against slavery.

1823
The Champlain Canal opens, connecting Lake Champlain with New York's Hudson River.

1837
John Deere patents the first steel plow.

1864
Confederate troops stage the Saint Albans Raid during the Civil War.

1900

1918
Vermont women vote in town elections for the first time.

1923
Calvin Coolidge of Plymouth Notch becomes the 30th U.S president.

124

U.S. Events

1929
The stock market crashes, plunging the United States more deeply into the Great Depression.

1941–45
The United States engages in World War II.

1950–53
The United States engages in the Korean War.

1964–73
The United States engages in the Vietnam War.

Madeleine Kunin

1991
The United States and other nations engage in the brief Persian Gulf War against Iraq.

2001
Terrorists attack the United States on September 11.

2003
The United States and coalition forces invade Iraq.

2008
The United States elects its first African American president, Barack Obama.

Vermont Events

1927
Vermont suffers the worst floods in its history.

1962
Philip H. Hoff becomes the first Democrat elected governor of Vermont since 1853.

1965
Redistricting gives Vermont cities more power in state government.

1968
Vermont bans billboards along its highways.

1970
Vermont limits developments that could harm the state's environment.

1984
Madeleine Kunin is elected the first female governor of Vermont.

2000

2004
Environmentalists halt construction of a highway around Burlington.

2011
Tropical Storm Irene causes extensive flooding in Vermont.

GLOSSARY

★ ★ ★

abolitionists people who were opposed to slavery and worked to end it

acid rain pollution that falls to the earth in the form of precipitation

alliance an association among groups that benefits all the members

amendment a change to a law or legal document

archaeologists people who study the remains of past human societies

clear-cutting a type of logging in which all of the trees in an area are cut down

constitution a written document that contains all the governing principles of a state or country

endangered at risk of becoming extinct

erosion the gradual wearing away of rock or soil by physical breakdown, chemical solution, or water

invasive species wildlife that is not native to a region and harms native plants or animals

machine tools mechanical devices used to manufacture metal machine parts

missionaries people who are sent to foreign lands to try to convert others to a religion

plantation a large farm, usually raising one main crop

quarrying extracting stone or minerals from an open-pit mine

redistrict to divide into new legislative districts

refugees people who flee their country to escape war, disease, persecution, or other circumstances

republic a nation in which the supreme power rests with citizens who can vote

sedition conduct or language that stirs up feelings against lawful authority

strike an organized refusal to work, usually as a sign of protest about working conditions

suffragette a woman in the early 1900s who worked for women's right to vote

textile cloth or fabric that is woven, knitted, or otherwise manufactured

threatened likely to become endangered in the foreseeable future

tributaries smaller rivers that flow into a larger river

unions organizations formed by workers to try to improve working conditions and wages

wood pulp ground-up chips or strips of wood

FAST FACTS

State Symbols

Statehood date	March 4, 1791, the 14th state
Origin of state name	From the French words *verts* (green) and *monts* (mountain)
State capital	Montpelier
State nickname	Green Mountain State
State motto	"Freedom and Unity"
State bird	Hermit thrush
State butterfly	Monarch butterfly
State animal	Morgan horse
State amphibian	Northern leopard frog
State flower	Red clover
State fish	Brook trout and walleye
State insect	Honeybee
State soil	Turnbridge soil series
State fossil	White whale
State rocks	Granite, marble, and slate
State mineral	Talc
State song	"These Green Mountains"
State tree	Sugar maple
State fair	Rutland (early September)

State seal

Geography

Total area; rank	9,616 square miles (24,905 sq km); 45th
Land; rank	9,217 square miles (23,872 sq km); 43rd
Water; rank	400 square miles (1,036 sq km); 46th
Inland water; rank	400 square miles (1,036 sq km); 41st
Geographic center	In Washington County, 3 miles (5 km) east of Roxbury
Latitude	42°44' N to 45°0'43" N
Longitude	71°28' W to 73°26' W
Highest point	Mount Mansfield, 4,393 feet (1,339 m), located in Lamoille County
Lowest point	Lake Champlain, 95 feet (29 m)

Largest city	Burlington
Counties	14
Longest river	Otter Creek, 100 miles (161 km)

Population

Population; rank (2010 census)	625,741; 49th
Density (2010 census)	68 persons per square mile (26 per sq km)
Population distribution (2010 census)	39% urban, 61% rural
Ethnic distribution (2010 census)	White persons: 94.3%
	Persons reporting two or more races: 1.6%
	Hispanic persons: 1.5%
	Asian persons: 1.3%
	Black persons: 0.9%
	American Indian and Alaska Native persons: 0.3%
	Persons of other races 0.1%

Weather

Record high temperature	107°F (42°C) at Vernon on July 7, 1912
Record low temperature	−50°F (−46°C) at Bloomfield on December 30, 1933
Average July temperature, Burlington	71°F (22°C)
Average January temperature, Burlington	19°F (−7°C)
Average yearly precipitation, Burlington	37 inches (94 cm)

State flag

STATE SONG

★ ★ ★

"These Green Mountains"

In 1998, the Vermont General Assembly directed the Vermont Arts Council to appoint a panel to recommend a new state song. "Hail, Vermont," the old state song, was considered difficult to sing. The council established a competition, and the winner was "These Green Mountains" by Diane B. Martin. It was named the official state song in 2000.

These green hills and silver waters
Are my home—they belong to me.
And to all of her sons and daughters
May they be strong and forever free.

Let us live to protect her beauty
And look with pride on the golden dome.
They say home is where the heart is.
These green mountains are my home.

These green mountains are my home.

NATURAL AREAS AND HISTORIC SITES

National Scenic Trail

About 150 miles (240 km) of the 2,184-mile (3,515 km) *Appalachian National Scenic Trail* passes through Vermont, traversing across the state's rugged hills and valleys.

National Historical Park

Vermont's *Marsh-Billings-Rockefeller National Historical Park* details the history of conservation and land stewardship in the United States. Visitors can walk through one of Vermont's most beautiful landscapes, under the shade of sugar maples and 400-year-old hemlocks, across covered bridges, and alongside rambling stone walls.

National Forest

The *Green Mountain National Forest*, in southwestern and west-central Vermont, provides scenic views and beautiful hiking trails.

State Parks and Forests

Vermont's state forest system maintains more than 50 state park and recreation areas, including *Fort Dummer State Park*, which was a British fort built in 1724 by the colonial militia of Massachusetts, and *Wilgus State Park*, which was constructed by the Civilian Conservation Corps during the Great Depression.

Emerald Lake State Park

SPORTS TEAMS

★ ★ ★

NCAA Teams (Division I)

University of Vermont *Catamounts*

A University of Vermont soccer player heads the ball.

CULTURAL INSTITUTIONS

Libraries

The *Bailey/Howe Library at the University of Vermont* (Burlington) holds the state's largest book collection.

The *Vermont State Library* (Montpelier) and the Vermont State Historical Society Library (Montpelier) have fine collections on the state's history.

Museums

The *Bennington Museum* (Bennington) has collections featuring early American glassware, pottery, and flags.

The *Henry Sheldon Museum of Vermont History* (Middlebury) houses early documents relating to Vermont's history, as well as portraits and household furnishings.

The *Shelburne Museum* (Shelburne) contains a wide variety of American art and historical artifacts.

The *Abenaki Tribal Museum* (Swanton) has exhibits about Abenaki history and culture.

The *Montshire Museum of Science* (Norwich) features displays about animals, astronomy, light, motion, and much more.

Performing Arts

The *Vermont Symphony Orchestra* (Burlington) brings symphonic music to large performance halls, schools, and rural farms and lakesides.

The *Vermont Opera Theater* (Montpelier) showcases opera and other musical performances by local professionals.

Universities and Colleges

In 2011, Vermont had 5 public and 17 private institutions of higher learning.

ANNUAL EVENTS

January–March

Vermont Farm Show in Essex Junction (January)

Vermont Flower Show in Essex Junction (February/March)

Town Meeting Day throughout the state (first Tuesday in March)

Antiquarian Spring Book Fair in Burlington (March)

April–June

Sugar Slalom in Stowe (April)

Vermont Maple Festival in St. Albans (April)

Vermont Dairy Festival in Enosburg Falls (June)

Vermont Quilt Festival in Essex Junction (late June/ early July)

July–September

Arts Festival on the Green in Middlebury (July)

Barre Heritage Festival and Homecoming Days in Barre (July)

County fairs in Barton, Bradford, Essex Junction, Lyndonville, Rutland, and Tunbridge (August–September)

Society of Animal Artists Exhibition in Bennington (September–October)

Foliage festivals statewide (late September–October)

October–December

Quilt Show in Shelburne (October)

Jeh Kulu's Annual Dance and Drum Festival in Burlington (November)

Holiday Lighting Ceremony in Burlington (November)

Country Christmas Open House in Waitsville (December)

Alpacas at the Vermont Farm Show

BIOGRAPHICAL DICTIONARY

Ethan Allen See page 39.

Trey Anastasio (1964–) is a songwriter, guitarist, and singer who is a longtime member of the rock band Phish. He is from Burlington.

Chester A. Arthur See page 91.

Warren Austin (1877–1962) was a senator from Vermont (1931–1946) and a U.S. ambassador to the United Nations (1946–1953).

Mary Azarian (1940–) is a printmaker and children's book illustrator who lives in Plainfield. She illustrated the 1999 book *Snowflake Bentley*, which won the Caldecott Medal for best picture book of the year.

Arthur Scott Bailey (1877–1949), a graduate of the University of Vermont, wrote more than 40 children's books. His stories took place in the animal, bird, and insect worlds, teaching about nature while telling engaging tales. He was born in St. Albans.

Consuelo N. Bailey See page 64.

Orson Bean (1928–) is a TV and movie actor. He was born in Burlington.

Wilson "Snowflake" Bentley (1865–1931), born in Jericho, was one of the first photographers of snowflakes. He created a process that enabled him to photograph them before they melted.

Richard Brewer (1850–1878) was a cowboy and lawman in the Old West. Born in St. Albans, he led a posse called the Regulators that hunted outlaws in New Mexico.

Jeanne Brink See page 79.

Pearl S. Buck

Pearl S. Buck (1892–1973) was an author whose best-known work, *The Good Earth*, is about family life in a Chinese village. She won both a Pulitzer Prize and a Nobel Prize for her writings. She had a home in Danby.

Samuel de Champlain (c.1567–1635) was a French explorer, navigator, and mapmaker. In 1609, he became the first European to reach Vermont.

Thomas Chittenden (1730–1797) was Vermont's first governor, serving from 1791 to 1797. Before that, he was governor of the Vermont Republic (1778–1789 and 1790–1791).

Barbara Ann Cochran (1951–) is a member of the Cochran family of skiers. Her parents ran a ski area in Richmond, and Barbara Ann and her three siblings were all members of the U.S. Ski Team in the late 1960s and early 1970s. Barbara Ann won a gold medal in the 1972 Winter Olympics.

Edmund "Tad" Coffin (1955–) is an equestrian, or horseback rider, and saddle maker. In 1976, he became the first American to win the Olympic gold medal in the three-day individual equestrian event. He rode his mare, Bally Cor. He lived in Strafford for many years.

Ben Cohen (1951–), with his partner, Jerry Greenfield, is the cofounder of Ben & Jerry's ice cream, based in Burlington. Born in New York, he moved to Vermont in the 1970s.

Calvin Coolidge See page 91.

Thomas Davenport (1802–1851) was an inventor who devised the electric motor in Brandon in 1837. He also invented electric trains. He was born in Williamstown.

Howard Dean (1948–) is a politician and a doctor who served as Vermont's governor (1991–2002) and chairman of the Democratic National Committee (2005–2009). In 2004, he was a candidate for the Democratic presidential nomination. Born in New York, he moved to Vermont in 1978.

John Deere

John Deere (1804–1886) was a blacksmith who invented the steel plow in 1837. He founded Deere & Company, one of the world's largest makers of farm equipment. He was born in Rutland.

George Dewey (1837–1917) was a U.S. Navy officer who led the U.S. victory in the Battle of Manila Bay in the Philippines during the Spanish–American War (1898). He was the only officer ever named to the rank of Admiral of the Navy. He was born in Montpelier.

John Dewey (1859–1952) was a philosopher and educator who believed that students should learn by solving problems and doing practical things. His views on education changed many of the nation's school practices. He was born in Burlington.

Stephen A. Douglas (1813–1861) was a politician who held a series of seven debates with Abraham Lincoln when they were running for U.S. senator in Illinois. People across the nation closely followed the debates, which focused on the issue of slavery. Douglas was born in Brandon.

Howard Dean

Horace Greeley

Martin Henry Freeman (1826–1889) was the first African American president of a U.S. college. In 1856, he was named president of Pennsylvania's Allegheny Institute (later Avery College). He was born in Rutland.

Robert Frost See page 81.

Horace Greeley (1811–1872) was a politician and a newspaperman who was the editor of the *New York Tribune*. Born in New Hampshire, he moved to West Haven, Vermont, with his family at age 10 and worked for a newspaper printer in East Poultney.

Jerry Greenfield (1951–), with his partner, Ben Cohen, is the cofounder of Ben & Jerry's ice cream, based in Burlington. Born in New York, he moved to Vermont in the 1970s.

Grey Lock (c. 1670–1750) was an Abenaki leader who fought the British settlers.

Joy Hakim See page 82.

James Hartness (1861–1934) was an inventor whose innovations boosted the machine-tool industry in southeastern Vermont. He also served as Vermont's governor (1921–1923). Born in New York, he later settled in Springfield.

Lemuel Haynes See page 53.

Stephen Huneck (1948–2010) was a woodcarving artist and furniture maker who often depicted dogs in his artwork. Working from his St. Johnsbury, Vermont, studio, he created pieces of artwork that are in the collections of the Smithsonian Institution and the American Kennel Club.

Richard Morris Hunt (1827–1895) was an architect who designed many prominent buildings in the United States. His designs in New York City include the Tribune Building, the front of the Metropolitan Museum of Art, and the pedestal of the Statue of Liberty. He was born in Brattleboro.

William Morris Hunt (1824–1879), the brother of Richard Morris Hunt, was an artist who painted scenes of life in France as well as portraits and landscapes. He was born in Brattleboro.

John Irving (1942–) is a novelist whose works include *The Cider House Rules*, *The Hotel New Hampshire*, and *The World According to Garp*. Born in New Hampshire, he later settled in Dorset.

John Irving

Bill Koch (1955–) is a cross-country skier. In 1976, he became the first American to win an Olympic medal in cross-country skiing when he won the silver medal in the 30 km event. He was born in Brattleboro.

Madeleine Kunin See page 89.

Patrick Leahy See page 88.

Henry David Lee (1849–1928), born in central Vermont, founded the H.D. Lee Mercantile Company, which became famous for its Lee jeans.

Henry Leland (1843–1932) was an automotive inventor who founded the Cadillac and Lincoln automobile companies. Leland's groundbreaking engine designs were the first used by both makes of cars. He was born in Barton.

David Mamet (1947–) is an award-winning playwright whose works include *Glengarry Glen Ross* and *Speed-the-Plow*. He has also written and directed many films. He lives in Woodbury.

George Perkins Marsh See page 18.

Andrea Mead (1932–2009) was the first American to win two Olympic gold medals in alpine (downhill) skiing, winning the 1952 slalom and giant slalom events. She was born in Rutland County.

Justin Morgan (1747–1798) was a horse breeder who developed the Morgan horse breed from his horse named Figure. This compact, muscular horse is one of the first breeds to originate in the United States, and it is Vermont's state animal. Born in Massachusetts, Morgan later settled in Vermont.

Andrea Mead

Justin Morrill (1810–1898) was a U.S. senator and congressman from Vermont. He sponsored the Morrill Land-Grant College Act, which provided funding for public colleges in the United States. He was born in Strafford.

Levi P. Morton (1824–1920) was a business-person and politician who served as vice president under President Benjamin Harrison (1889–1893). He was born in Shoreham.

Elisha Otis See page 100.

Grace Paley (1922–2007) was a short story writer and poet whose work focused on the lives of average women. Her books include *The Little Disturbances of Man* and *Later the Same Day*. She lived in Thetford Hill.

Annette Parmalee See page 56.

Katherine Paterson (1932–) is a children's book author. Her award-winning books include *Jacob Have I Loved* and *Bridge to Terabithia*, which was made into a 2007 movie. She moved to Barre in 1986.

Moses Pendleton (1949–) is a choreographer, or composer of dances. His dance company, MOMIX, has toured the world with its performances combining light, shadow, music, and the human body. He was born and raised on a dairy farm in northern Vermont.

Russell Porter (1871–1949) explored the Arctic in the late 1890s and early 1900s alongside adventurer Robert Peary. He became an expert telescope maker and helped design what was then the largest telescope on Earth, at Mount Palomar in Pasadena, California. He was born in Springfield.

Annie Proulx (1935–) is a novelist and short story writer who lived in Vermont for more than 30 years. Her 1993 novel, *The Shipping News*, won the National Book Award and the Pulitzer Prize.

William Russell (1831–1899) was a paper manufacturer and a Massachusetts congressman. He was one of the first people to use wood pulp instead of rags to make paper. In 1870, he established the first wood-pulp paper mill in the United States at Bellows Falls. He was born in Wells River.

Bernard Sanders (1941–) has represented Vermont in both the U.S. House of Representatives (1991–2007) and the U.S. Senate (2007–). He is the longest-serving independent (neither Democratic nor Republican) member of Congress in U.S. history.

Patty Sheehan (1956–) is a professional golfer who has won several major championships. She was born in Middlebury.

Joseph Smith (1805–1844) was a religious leader who founded the Church of Jesus Christ of Latter-day Saints, also known as the Mormon Church. He was born in Sharon.

Aleksandr Solzhenitsyn (1918–2008) was a Russian author who exposed the Soviet labor camp system. His best-known work is *One Day in the Life of Ivan Denisovich*. He received the Nobel Prize in Literature in 1970. Exiled from Russia, he lived in Cavendish from 1976 to 1994.

Homer St. Francis See page 71.

Horace A. Tabor (1830–1899) was a "silver king" who made a fortune in the Colorado silver mines. He was born in Holland, Vermont.

Hannah Teter (1987–) is a snowboarder who won a gold medal at the 2006 Olympic Games. She is from Belmont.

Hannah Teter

Dorothy Thompson

Dorothy Thompson (1893–1961) was a leading journalist of the 1930s and 1940s. Her work raised awareness of the threat posed by German leader Adolf Hitler in the years before World War II. She lived in Barnard.

Ernest Thompson (1949–) is a playwright whose work includes *On Golden Pond*, which was made into a movie in 1981. He was born in Bellows Falls.

Alexander Twilight (1795–1857) was the first African American to earn a college degree and to be elected to public office in the United States. He was born in Corinth.

Rudy Vallée (1901–1986) was a singer, bandleader, and actor popular in the 1940s. He was born in Island Pond.

Henry Wells (1805–1878) was the founder of Wells & Co., a delivery company. It later merged with other companies to form the American Express Company. He was president of American Express from 1850 to 1868. He was born in Thetford.

Brigham Young (1801–1877) was the governor of Utah Territory and president of the Mormon Church. He was born in Whittingham.

Meeri Zetterstrom See page 23.

RESESOURCES

BOOKS

Nonfiction

Esty, Amos. *The Liberator: The Story of William Lloyd Garrison.* Greensboro, N.C.: Morgan Reynolds Publishing, 2010.

Fryer, Mary Beacock. *Champlain: Peacemaker and Explorer.* Toronto, Ontario, Can.: Dundurn Press, 2011.

Kavanagh, James. *Vermont Wildlife: An Introduction to Familiar Species.* Dunedin, Fla.: Waterford Press, 2008.

Miglorie, Catherine. *Vermont's Marble Industry.* Charleston, S.C.: Arcadia Publishing, 2013.

Sommers, Michael. *Vermont Past and Present.* New York: Rosen Central, 2010.

Fiction

Bruchac, Joseph. *Gluskabe and the Four Wishes.* New York: Cobblehill Books/Dutton, 1995.

Bruchac, Marge. *Malian's Song.* Middlebury: Vermont Folklife Center, 2006.

Fisher, Dorothy Canfield. *Understood Betsy.* New York: Henry Holt, 1917, 1999.

Walter, Mildred Pitts. *Alec's Primer.* Middlebury: Vermont Folklife Center, 2004.

Visit this Scholastic Web site for more information on Vermont:
www.factsfornow.scholastic.com
Enter the keyword **Vermont**

INDEX

★ ★ ★

Page numbers in *italics* indicate illustrations.

18th Amendment, 60
19th Amendment, *57*

Abenaki people, 26, 28–29, 29–
    30, 30–31, *31*, 35, 36, 37,
    38, *70*, 71, 79, *79*, 135
Abenaki Tribal Museum, 108
abolitionists, 51–52, *52*
Adams, John, 48
Addison, 29, 36, 110
African Americans, 41, 51, 52,
    53, 54, 64, 70, 106, 135,
    137
agriculture, 16, *16*, 19, 29, 42,
    47, 54, 57, *58*, 61, 62, 66,
    70, 75, 86, 95, 96, 99,
    101, *101*, *103*, 134
Alien and Sedition Acts, 48
Allen, Ethan, 39, *39*, *40*, 53, 87
Allen, Ira, 39
American Colonization Society, 51
American Precision Museum, 62,
    114
American Revolution. *See*
    Revolutionary War.
Anastasio, Trey, *80*, 133
Andover, 42
animal life, 14, 21–22, *21*, *22*,
    23, *24*, 25, 26, 29, 30, 42,
    43, *47*, *47*, 48, 62, 79,
    101, *101*, 109, 110, *110*,
    113, *113*
Archaic Period, 26
Arrowhead Mountain Lake, 23
art, 78–79, 114, 133, 135
Arthur, Chester A., 91, *91*
artifacts, 29, *29*, *31*, 109, 110
Asian Americans, *70*, 79
attorneys general, 89
Austin, Warren R., 133
automobiles, 56
Azarian, Mary, 133

Bailey, Arthur Scott, 133
Bailey, Consuelo N., 63, 64, *64*
Baker, Remember, 39

Barre, 16, 49, 54, 55, 72, 86,
    102
Battle of Bennington, 41, 115
Bean, Orson, 133
Bellows Falls, 54
Ben & Jerry's ice cream, *77*, *77*,
    99, 111, *111*, 134, 135
Bennington, 39, 41, 48, 51, 81,
    115
Bentley, Wilson "Snowflake", 133
birds, 21, 22, *22*, 113, 114, 115
Bloomfield, 18
bobcats, 21, *21*
Bolton, 55
border, 10, *10*
Bradford, *60*
Brandon, 52
Brattleboro, 36, 54, 78, 80
Bread Loaf writers' workshop, 75
Brewer, Richard, 133
Brink, Jeanne, *79*, 79
Bristol, 110
British settlers, 35–36, 37, 38
Brownington, 106
Buck, Pearl S., 133, *133*
Burgoyne, John, 41
Burke, 107
Burke Mountain, 107
Burlington, 12, 17, 71, 72, 73,
    73, 75, 80, *80*, 99, 108,
    109

Camel's Hump, 14
caribou, *24*, 25
Champlain Canal, 50
Champlain, Samuel de, *7*, *32*,
    33, 133
Champlain Valley, 12, 13, 17–
    18, 19, 101, 102
Champ (sea serpent), 17
Chaplin, Charlie, 60
Charlotte, 108
Chatham, *65*
cheese, 43, 49, 54, 76, 77,
    77, 99, 109, 110, 113
Chimney Point settlement, 35–36
Chimney Point State Historic Site,
    29
Chittenden, Thomas, 133

Church Street Marketplace, 109
Civilian Conservation Corps
    (CCC), 61
Civil War, 52–53, *53*, 87
climate, 18–19, *19*, 20, 23, 26,
    61, 65, 67
clothing, 29, 48, 60, 79
coastline, 17–18
Cochran, Barbara Ann, 133
Coffin, Edmund "Tad," 134
Cohen, Ben, 111, 134
common crackers, *77*
common terns, 22
Concord Corner, 75
coniferous trees, 20
Connecticut River, 10, *10*, 16,
    28, 36, *36*, 78
Coolidge, Calvin, 59, 60, 91,
    91, 112, *112*
Cornish Colony, 78–79counties,
    92, 93
Cowasuck people, 28
crafts, 29, *78*, 79, *79*, 106,
    108, 110, 112, 113
crops, 16, *16*, 17, 19, 26, 29,
    96, 101
crushed stone, 102

dairy farming, 47, 49, 54, *58*,
    62, 99, 101
dance, 60, 79, 80, 136
Davenport, Thomas, 134
Dean, Howard, 134, *134*
deciduous trees, 20
Declaration of Independence, 40
Deere, John, 134, *134*
Democratic Party, 63, 88, 134
Department of Fish and Wildlife,
    23
Derby Line, 106
Dewey, George, 134
Dewey, John, 134
Dillon, John, 93
dimension stone, 102
diseases, 54, 55
district courts, 91
Dorset, 48
Douglas, Stephen A., 134
Drennan, Bessie, 78

E. & T. Fairbanks and Company Scale Manufactury, *55*
education, 54, *75*, *75*, 89, 99, 134
elections, 48, 56, 57, 63, 64, *84*, 85, 87, 88, 89, 90
electricity, 99, 134
elevation, 9, *11*, 14, *14*, 17
Ely Copper Mines, 55
endangered species, 22
Environmental Control Act, 66
environmental protection, 18, 22–23, 65–66, *66*, 67, 74
Essex Junction, 72
ethnic groups, 69, 70, *71*
Eureka Schoolhouse, 114
European exploration, *32*, 33, *34*, 36–37, 133
European settlers, 17, 30, 33, 35–36, *36*, 37, *37*, 38
executive branch of government, 86, 88–89, 90

Fairfield, *58*
Fair Haven, 48, 102
Fair Haven Gazette newspaper, 48
family courts, 91
Farm Security Administration, *60*
ferns, 20
ferries, 108, *108*
Ferrisburgh, 52, 54
fiddlehead ferns, 20
Fisher, Dorothy Canfield, 82
Fitzgerald, F. Scott, 60
flooding, 23, 61, 111
folk art, 78, 79
food processing, 99, *99*
foods, 22, 26, 29, 30, 43, 49, 60, 61, 62, 76, *77*, *77*, 99, *99*, 102
forests, 7, 9, 13, 14, 16, 18, 20, 21, *21*, 22, 23, 26, 29, 35, *38*, 48, 83, *83*, 95, 112, 114
Fort Dummer, 36
Fort Sainte Anne settlement, 35
Fort Ticonderoga, 39–40, *40*, 53
Freeman, Martin Henry, 52, 135
French and Indian War, 37–38, *38*
French Canadians, 70, 80
French exploration, *32*, 33, 133
French settlers, 33, 35, 37, 38
Frost, Robert, 75, 81, *81*

Fuller, Ida May, 61
fur trade, 35, *35*, 36–37

Garfield, James, 91
Garrison, William Lloyd, 51, *52*
General Assembly, 87, 95
Gershwin, George, 60
glaciers, 12
Glover, 106
governors, 39, 51, 63, 64, 64, 87, 88, *88*, 89, *89*, 91, 133, 134, 137
Grand Isle, 108
granite, 13, 16, 49, 54, 55, 79, 86, 98, 102
Great Depression, 61
Greeley, Horace, 135, *135*
Greenfield, Jerry, 111, 135
Green Mountain Boys, 39–40, 40, 48, 53, 87
Green Mountain National Forest, 14, 23, 114
Green Mountains, *8*, 9, 12, 13–14, 16, 18–19, 36, 63, 65, 81, *83*, 115
Grey Lock (Abenaki leader), 37, 135
Guilford, 51

Hakim, Joy, 82, *82*
Hall of Flags, 87
Harding, Warren G., 59, 91
Harrison, Benjamin, 136
Hartness, James, 135
Haynes, Lemuel, 52, 53, *53*
hiking, 14, 18, 83, 105, 111, 113, 114, 115, *115*
Hoff, Philip, 63
Holhut, Randolph T., 93
horses, *42*, 56, 108, 110, *110*, 136
housing, 28–29, *43*, 66, 74, 89
Hubbard Park, 87
Hubbardton, 40
Huneck, Stephen, 107, 135
Hunt, Richard Morris, 78, 135
Hunt, William Morris, 78, 135

immigrants, 48, 54
independence, 41, 42
insect life, 22
interstate highways, *104*
invasive species, 21–22
Iroquois Nation, 38
Irving, John, 135, *135*
Island Pond, 106

Island Pond Lake, 106
islands, 18, 35
Isle La Motte, 35

Jackson, Horatio Nelson, 56
Jarvis, William, 47
Jay, 106
jobs, 54–55, 61, 62–63, 64, 71, *100*
Journal of the Times newspaper, 51
judicial branch of government, 86, 90, 91

Killington Peak, 14
Koch, Bill, 82, 135
Kunin, Madeleine, 64, *64*, 89, *89*

labor strikes, 55
labor unions, 55
Lake Champlain, 7, 9, 10, 12, 14, 17–18, 21, 22, 26, *28*, 33, 35, 39, 50, 108, *108*, 109, 110
Lake Champlain Chocolates, 99, *99*
Lake Memphremagog, 13, *13*, 17
Lamoille River, 14
land area, 9, 12
languages, 26, 70, 71, 73, 76
laws, 23, 41, 56, 66, 85, 87, 89
Leahy, Patrick, 63, 88, *88*
Lee, Henry David, 135
legislative branch of government, 51, 56, 63, 86, 87–88, 89, 90, 91, 94, 95
Leland, Henry, 136
lieutenant governors, 63, 64, 88–89
Lincoln, Abraham, 134
literature, 60, 81–82, 133, 135, 136
livestock, 16, 17, *42*, 47, *47*, 48, 54, 62, 79, 101, *101*, 113, *113*
local government, 93
logging industry, 14, 22, 23, 47–48, 54
longhouses, 29
Long Trail, 14, 115, *115*
lumber industry. *See* logging industry.
lunar calendar, 28
Lyndonville, *67*
Lyon, Matthew, 48

machine-tool manufacturing, 54, 62, 114
Mamet, David, 136
Man and Nature (George Perkins Marsh), 18
Manchester, 17, 82
Manchester Center, 114
manufacturing, 50, 54, *55*, 56–57, 61, 62, 63, 99–101
Maple Grove Farms, 107
Maple Nut Bars recipe, *77*
maple syrup, 20, 30, *37*, 69, 76, *76*, *77*, *77*, 102, 108, 113
maps
    agriculture, *103*
    counties, *92*
    European exploration, *34*
    interstate highways, *104*
    mining, *103*
    Montpelier, *87*
    national parks, *15*
    Native Americans, *27*
    population density, *72*
    statehood, *46*
    territory, *46*
    topography, *11*
marble, 17, 48, 49, *50*, 54, 79, 87, 102, 112
marble quarrying, 17, 48, *50*, 54
marine life, 21, 115
Marlboro, *75*, 80, 115
Marlboro College, *75*, 83
Marlboro Music Festival, *75*, 80
Marsh, George Perkins, 18, *18*, 112
Marsh, Rodney, 52
Mead, Andrea, 82, 136, *136*
Memphre (sea monster), 17
Merino sheep, 47, *47*
Meyer, William, 63
Middlebury, 48, 110
Middlebury College, 52, 53, *75*, *75*, 82
mining, 54, 55, 74, 99, 102, *103*
missionaries, 35
Missisquoi people, 26, 70, 71
Missisquoi River, 14, 28
Mohican people, 26
Montpelier, 16, 73, *76*, 86, *86*, 87, *87*, 111
moose callers, 29, *29*
Morgan Horse Farm, 110, *110*
Morgan horses, 110, *110*, 136

Morgan, Justin, 136
Morrill, Justin, 136
Morrill Land–Grant College Act, 136
Morton, Levi P., 136
Mount Ellen, 14
Mount Equinox, 17
Mount Mansfield, 9, 12, 14, *14*, 111
Mount Tambora (Indonesia), 19
Mount Wilson, 14
museums, 29, 54, 62, 78, 79, 98, 106, *106*, 107, 108, 109, 110, 111, 112, 113, *113*, 114, *114*, 115
music, 60, 75, 79, 80, *80*, 112, 133, 137

national parks, *15*
National Wildlife Federation, 23
Native Americans, 17, 24, 25, 26, *27*, 28–29, *28*, 29–30, 30–31, *31*, 35, *35*, 37, *37*, 38, 70, 71, 79, *79*, 110, 135
Newbury, 28
New Deal, 60, 61
New France colony, 33
New Hampshire Grants, 39
North Danville, 107
Northeast Highlands, 12, 13
Northeast Kingdom, 16
North Hero, 108
Norwich, 113

Old Constitution House, 40, 114
Old Round Church, 109
Olympic Games, 82, 107, 133, 134, 135, 136, *136*, 137, *137*
ospreys, 22, *22*, 23, 115
Otis Elevator Company, 100
Otis, Elisha Graves, 100, *100*
Otter Creek River, 12

Paleo-Indians, *24*, 25
Paley, Grace, 136
paper manufacturing, 48, 137
Parmalee, Annette, 56, *56*
Parrish, Maxfield, 78, *78*, 114
Paterson, David, *81*
Paterson, Katherine, 81, *81*, 136
Pendleton, Moses, 136
Pennacook people, 26
Phish (rock band), 80, *80*, 133
Pittsford, 112

plant life, 20, 23, 25, 26, 29, 30, 101
Plymouth, 112
Plymouth Notch, 59, 91, 112
pollution, 23, 66
population, 47, 63, 64, 65, *72*, 73, *74*, 86
Porter Music Box Company, 112
Porter, Russell, 136
Prince, Abijah, 51
Proctor, 54, 112
Proulx, Annie, 136

quarrying, 17, 48–49, *50*, 54, *55*, 102
Quechee, 113
Quechee Gorge, 113

railroads, 55, 115
Randolph, 112
recipe, *77*
refugees, 71
religion, 30, 31, *31*, 35, 53
reptilian life, 109, 115
Republican Party, 63
Republic of New Connecticut, 41
Revolutionary War, 39, 41, 48, 51, 87, 110, 115
Richmond, 109
Ripton, 75, 81
roadways, 66, 67, 85, *104*
Roaring Twenties, 60
Robinson, Rachel, 52, 54
Robinson, Rowland, 52, 54
Rock of Ages granite quarry, 102
Rokeby Museum, 54
Roosevelt, Franklin D., 61
Royce, Robert, 63
rural areas, 54, 63, 73–74, 75, 78, 79, 81, 99, 101, 113
Russell, William, 137
Rutland, 17, 69, 72

sachem (Abenaki spiritual leader), 31, *31*
Saint Albans, 54, 108
Saint Albans Raid, 53, 54
Saint Johnsbury, 54, *55*, 107
Sanders, Bernard, 137
secretary of state, 89
service industries, 97, 98–99, *98*
settlers, 17, 30, 33, 35–36, *36*, 36–37, *37*, 38, 39, 41, 42–43, *42*, 43
Shaftsbury, 81
Sheehan, Patty, 137

Shelburne, 100, 109, *109*
Shelburne Museum, 79, 109
shipwrecks, 108, 110
Shumlin, Peter, 67, *88*
Sims, Stella Hackel, 63–64
skiing, 14, 19, 63, 66, 68, 74, 82, 83, *83*, 98, 106, 107, 111, 114, 133, 135, 136, *136*
slate quarrying, 49, 54, 102
slavery, 41, 51, 52, 54, 86, 134
Smith, Joseph, 137
snowmobiling, 106
Social Security, 61
Sokoki people, 26, 28, 70, 71
Solzhenitsyn, Aleksandr, 137
South Burlington, 72
South Hero Island, 18
Spanish–American War, 134
sports, 14, 82, 83, 106, 107, 133, 135, 136, *136*, 137, *137*
Springfield, 54, 62, 114
Stamford, 115
Stark, John, 41
state auditor, 89
state capital, 16, 73, 86, *87*
state capitol, 86, *86*, 87
state constitution, 40, 41, 44, 86, 114
state flag, 94, *94*
statehood, 45, 46, 47, 86
state motto, 69, 95, *95*
state name, 7
state nickname, 14
state seal, 94, 95, *95*
state supreme court, 91
state treasurer, 89
state tree, 20, *20*
St. Francis, Homer, 71
Stowe, *68*, 82, 111
suffrage movement, 56, *57*
Sugarbush Farm, 113
sugar maple (state tree), 20, *20*, 30
Sunderland, 51
superior court, 91
Swanton, 28, 70, 108

Tabor, Horace A., 137
Taconic Mountains, 12, 13, 17, 36
tectonic plates, 12
tepees, 29
Terry, Lucy, 51

Teter, Hannah, 82, 137, *137*
textile industry, 48, 62
theater, 80, 106
Thompson, Dorothy, 137, *137*
Thompson, Ernest, 137
threatened species, 22
timber industry. *See* logging industry.
tourism, 56, 63, 65, 66, 82, 83, 98
Town Meeting Day, 85, 93
transportation, 22, 50, 56, 108
Twilight, Alexander, 52, 106, 137

Underground Railroad, 52
University of Vermont, 75, 80, 82, 110
U.S. Congress, 48, 87, 90, 137
U.S. Constitution, 57, 60
U.S. House of Representatives, 63, 90, 137
U.S. Senate, 88, 90, 133, 136
U.S. Supreme Court, 63, 64

Valentino, Rudolph, 60
Vallée, Rudy, 137
Valley of Vermont. *See* Vermont Valley.
Vermont Anti-Slavery Society, 51
Vermonters for a Clean Environment, 74
Vermont Institute of Natural Science (VIN S) Nature Center, 113
Vermont Lowland. *See* Champlain Valley.
Vermont Natural Resources Council, 23
Vermont Piedmont. *See* Western New England Upland.
Vermont Republic, 41, 133
Vermont State House, 87, 111
Vermont Symphony Orchestra, 80
Vermont Teddy Bear Company, 100–101, *101*, 109
Vermont Theatre Company, 80
Vermont Valley, 13, 17, 36, 102
Vermont Wildflower Farm, 108
Vermont Youth Orchestra, 80, *80*
Vernon, 18, 19
Vittum, Margaret, 93
voting rights, 41, 56, *57*, *57*, 86

Wabanaki Confederacy, 26
Walloomsac River, 48

Warner, Moses, 42
Warner, Seth, 39
Waterbury, 99, 111
Wells, Henry, 137
Western New England Upland, 13, 16
West Rutland, *47*
wigwams, 28–29
wildflowers, 20, 108
wildlife. *See* animal life; insect life; marine life; plant life; reptilian life.
Windsor, 40, 41, 54, 62, 79, 114
Windsor–Cornish Covered Bridge, *10*
Windsor Tavern, 40
Winooski River, 14, 61
Winooski River Valley, 61
women, 29, 42, 43, 56, 57, *57*, 60, 62, 64, 89
Woodbury, 78
Woodland Period, 26
Woodstock, *19*, 112, 113
World War I, 57
World War II , 61–62, 64, 137

Young, Brigham, 137

zebra mussels, 21–22
Zetterstrom, Meeri, 23, *23*

AUTHOR'S TIPS AND SOURCE NOTES

★   ★   ★

Two books give excellent accounts of the natural and cultural forces that shaped Vermont. They are *The Story of Vermont: A Natural and Cultural History* by Christopher McGrory Klyza and Stephen C. Trombulak and *Hands on the Land: A History of the Vermont Landscape* by Jan Albers. Another great book is *The Voice of the Dawn: An Autohistory of the Abenaki Nation* by Frederick Matthew Wiseman. It treats the reader to fascinating insights into Abenaki history and culture.